The Old Testament in Theology and Teaching

Essays in Honor of
Kay Fountain

Edited by Teresa Chai and Dave Johnson

WIPF & STOCK · Eugene, Oregon

Wipf and Stock Publishers
199 W 8th Ave, Suite 3
Eugene, OR 97401

The Old Testament in Theology and Teaching
Essays in Honor of Kay Fountain
By Chai, Teresa and Johnson, Dave
Copyright©2018 APTS Press
ISBN 13: 978-1-5326-4694-2
Publication date 1/17/2018
Previously published by APTS Press, 2018

This edition is published by Wipf and Stock Publishers under license from APTS Press.

CONTENT

i	*Foreword* John Carter
v	*Introduction* Teresa Chai and Dave Johnson Editors
1	*Kay Fountain: Historical-Biographical Sketch* Adelina C. Ladera
19	*Asian Theological Education: Now and Then* *An Asian Pentecostal Pastor-Educator's Survey of* *Theological Education* Tham Wan Yee
49	*Illuminating a Canaanite and Judahite Town:* *The Archaeological Background of Tel Burna* Itzhaq Shai with Chris McKinny, Benjamin Yang, and Deborah Cassuto
69	*How Can a Person Read Esther?* Tim Bulkeley
81	*Navigating the Empire: Esther as a Model of Marginalisation* Jacqueline Grey
95	*Gideon and the Angel of the Lord: An Anthropological* *Perspective: Judges 6:11-40* Dave Johnson
115	*Tragedy of Spirit-Empowered Heroes: A Close Look at Samson* *and Saul* Wonsuk Ma
133	*The Charismatic and Non-Charismatic Roles of the Spirit in* *Isaiah 11:1-5* Lian Sian Mung

155 *Wise Participation in the Divine Life: Lessons from the Life of Daniel*
Tim Meadowcroft

175 *Old Testament Pedagogy on Mission*
Teresa Chai

191 *Profiles of Contributors*

FOREWORD

It is my pleasure to write the Foreword for this *Festschrift*: *The Old Testament in Theology and Teaching,* honoring Dr. Allison Kay Fountain (known by her colleagues and friends as "Kay" and by her students as "Dr. Kay"). I first became aware of her in 1987 while I was serving as Dean of the College for International Correspondence Institute (ICI – now Global University), when it was located in Brussels, Belgium. Each year the accreditation commission for ICI (the National Home Study Council—NHSC) honored an outstanding student at each academic level that it accredited, and ICI had nominated Kay Fountain for this honor since she had just completed the B.A. in Bible and Theology with an outstanding academic record. She was selected by NHSC as the baccalaureate level recipient for that year from among the world-wide graduates of its accredited schools. The honor included a trip to the NHSC headquarters in Washington D.C. for the award presentation. Since she was travelling from her home in New Zealand, she arranged to make a stop in Brussels to visit the ICI headquarters. Although I was travelling at the time of her visit, I received reports indicating she was a wonderful representative of ICI's academic programs.

A few years later, when I was serving as APTS Academic Dean, I was surprised to learn that she had applied for admission to our M.A. program. It was my pleasure to have her as a student in several of my classes where she always received the highest grade. In fact, as she had done before, she achieved an outstanding academic record throughout her studies at APTS. After she completed the APTS M.Div. degree, she was invited to join the faculty development program by President Bill

Menzies while continuing her studies for the PhD, which she also completed in record time.

There is no questioning that Kay's academic career has been characterized by a pattern of excellence and exceptional achievement, culminating in her service to APTS as a faculty member for the past 22 years and as Academic Dean since 2012. But Kay's interests have not only been in the academic, but also in practical ministry as she has found time to serve the church and Bible school in Mongolia as a missionary educator and pastor, and to serve as pastor of an active church in Baguio, Philippines. Indeed, her ability to balance the academic with practical ministry and maintain a pattern of excellence in both is especially noteworthy. If that weren't enough, she also qualified herself as a Master scuba diver during recent years.

In keeping with the theme of this *Festschrift: The Old Testament in Theology and Teaching,* the included articles predominantly provide an Old Testament focus. Significantly, most have been written by Kay's current and former students and colleagues, both Western and Asian, including one by her PhD mentor, Dr. Tim Bulkeley. The topics range from studies of the book of Esther, the subject of Kay's own doctoral dissertation, to the consideration of aspects of work of the Holy Spirit in OT contexts (i.e. Wonsuk Ma and Lian Sian Mung). The volume leads off with a review of theological education in Asia by Tham Wan Yee, the current APTS President. Other articles discuss a variety of subjects relevant to Old Testament studies, including an archeological dig in Israel that Kay has participated in and an examination of missions teaching in the Old Testament. Together they provide reflections on a variety of topics that give insight into the scholarly concerns that were relevant to Kay's own teaching and research.

For anyone involved in higher education, and especially theological education, it is particularly gratifying to see students excel in their own right as they pursue God's leading in their lives. I can say without hesitation that Dr. A. Kay Fountain is one such student who took everything she was taught, magnified it through her own efforts and achieved noteworthy accomplishments as a teacher and church leader. At every level of both academic and practical ministry endeavor, she has excelled in her achievements. I know that future generations of her own students will reflect positively upon the influence she has had on their lives.

John F. Carter, PhD
President Emeritus
Asia Pacific Theological Seminary

Kay Fountain

Introduction

We are privileged to offer this festschrift honoring Dr. Kay Fountain, who for more than twenty years has served the Lord at the Asia Pacific Theological Seminary (APTS), in Baguio City, Philippines, first as a student, then as a faculty member and finally as the Academic Dean. Our hope is that this book will reflect her passion for teaching and understanding the Old Testament, which has instilled in her students that kind of passion for the ministry as well.

Providing us with a personal insight into Kay's life, her classmate and friend, Dr. Adelina Ladera writes her autobiography. Beginning from some childhood anecdotes, Ladera walks us through the rooms of Fountain's life with great skill and humor. Clearly, Fountain has led a colorful life with many interesting experiences, which have shaped her to be who she is today. Included are stories from Fountain's year as a missionary in Mongolia, her 10 years as senior pastor of International Praise Centre, Baguio, as well as her years at APTS.

Next is an article by the President of APTS himself, Rev. Yee Tham Wan, who challenges us to consider how theological education has developed over the years in Asia. Approaching this from both an educator's and a pastor's perspective, he deals with both the theoretical and the practical aspects of theological training in Asia.

For several years now, Fountain has been making an annual trip to Israel, joining an archaeological dig at a place called Tel Burna. This chapter is written by her co-workers there, particularly Dr. Itzhaq Shai.

It includes the site's background, which sheds historical light not only on this place, but also helps us appreciate the geographical setting of a typical Canaanite and Judahite town.

Dr. Tim Bulkeley was Fountain's mentor for her PhD in Old Testament Studies of the Book of Esther. As such, his is a most appropriate article on how a person can read this historical book of the Bible. Bulkeley refers to his time of mentoring Fountain, particularly her reading of the text as a woman. Following up on this, Dr. Jacqueline Grey, an esteemed Associate Professor of the Old Testament, teaching in Alphacrucis College, Australia, writes on how to navigate the contextual background of Esther. Grey proposes that the Book of Esther is about marginalization. She also deals with the modeling and mentoring aspects of Esther, paralleling this with Fountain's ministry and inspiration to other female educators, missionaries and ministers who have come after her, including Grey herself.

The next few chapters are about other Old Testament characters. Dr. Dave Johnson, a colleague of Fountain's at APTS, writes from a missiological point of view focusing in on Gideon and the Angel of the LORD as seen in Judges 6:11-40. He gives a fresh way of looking at this passage anthropologically. Johnson has been researching animistic cultures for over twenty years and applies the principles from the Gideon narrative to the Asian context. He also deals with the patron-client relationships seen Judges 6 and in Asian cultures. Then, taking two Bible characters who may be seen as "not-the-best" role models, Dr. Wonsuk Ma, one of Fountain's former colleagues, helps us learn from the tragic narratives of Samson and Saul (Judges 13 and 1 Samuel 10). These were Spirit-Empowered men who failed and yet there was still a glimmer of hope in their stories. This is a caution to contemporary Pentecostal leaders not to fall into the common trap of pride. Ma's article deals with the importance for Charismatic leaders of morality and a strong spiritual life.

Dr. Lian Sian Mung, Fountain's student in Biblical Hebrew and exegesis, has gone on to be an Old Testament scholar in his own right. He gives us insights into the roles of the Spirit found in Isaiah 11:1-5. He divides the roles of the Spirit into two categories of "charismatic" meaning the empowerment for the ministerial task and the "non-charismatic" meaning the character of the person who obeys God being in line with His intention. Then, Dr. Tim Meadowcroft writes about life lessons from Daniel especially on how to wisely participate in life in God. The picture that Meadowcroft paints is that of "earth touching heaven," interactions of the eschaton with the "here and now," and the wisdom of God being within reach but also hidden.

The final chapter is written by Dr. Teresa Chai, the successor to Fountain in the APTS Academic Dean position. Fountain has been her boss, local senior pastor, dive instructor, friend and sister in Christ. Chai, in her chapter, looks at the pedagogy of missions in the Old Testament, walking through sections where God clearly teaches His people about His mission among the nations. Special attention is given to pedagogical and missiological implications for the Church today.

Finally, we would like to express a word of appreciation to the Assemblies of God of New Zealand, under the leadership of their general superintendent, Rev. Iliafi Esera, for providing funding for this project.

We hope that the different chapters in this book will warm your hearts and give you new insights into the Old Testament in theology and teaching. You are welcome to contact us with questions and comments through www.apts.edu.

Sincerely in Christ,

Teresa Chai, PhD and Dave Johnson, DMiss
Editors

KAY FOUNTAIN: HISTORICAL-BIOGRAPHICAL SKETCH

by Adelina C. Ladera

Introduction

As in Scripture, God has arranged events in our lives to fulfill His purposes. Our destiny is laid before us even before we were born. This is true of Kay Fountain, an exceptional achiever who, although reluctant at first, was convinced by God that she could do exploits through Him.

This brief overview of Kay's life will include her childhood upbringing, ministry call and what the Lord has accomplished through her in many roles. Included are her achievements as an outstanding student, missionary-instructor and administrator at the Asia Pacific Theological Seminary (APTS), as well as her work as a teacher and minister in Mongolia and in Baguio City, Philippines, where she serves as senior pastor of International Praise Center (IPC).

In researching Kay's life, the author interviewed and emailed questionnaires to colleagues, staff, students, pastors, church leaders, family, friends and roommates whose lives have been touched, influenced and impacted by her life and ministry.

Childhood Upbringing

Kay had a remarkable childhood upbringing. She was the youngest among three girls of her parents, John and Nan Fountain,[1] who greatly influenced her. Two family traditions were especially significant to Kay. Each summer, starting when she was only eighteen months old, the whole family went camping. Camping trained her to get out of her comfort zone and prepared her for ministry in the mountains and remote places. Another important tradition that her father started during her early teens, was the daily Bible reading and prayer at their breakfast table. There were no commentaries, just the unadulterated Word of God. It gave her an incredible knowledge of the Bible while growing up.[2]

Church was an integral part of the Fountain family life. They attended a Presbyterian church and during camping holidays, when there was none available, they went to other churches like the Anglican or Methodist.[3] Kay's father was an exemplary Christian man. The church that they attended until she was five years old was started by a meeting in their home. Her father served as a deacon or elder in all the churches they attended. Kay occasionally won prizes for memorizing Bible verses at Scripture Union contests when she was five to nine years old.[4]

Kay's mother, who worked in a sewing factory before her marriage, taught the girls how to sew. At the age of twelve, Kay was designing and sewing her own dresses.[5] She recalled how her Mom trained them to become young adults:

> By the time we were ten, we had to make up a menu, go with her to buy all the ingredients and make the meal for the whole family by ourselves. We shared the chores around the house and

---

[1] Kay Fountain, email to author, 25 November 2015.
[2] Kay Fountain, interview by author, 31 August 2015, APTS, Baguio City, Philippines, 1.
[3] Ibid., 4.
[4] Ibid., 1.
[5] Ibid., 6-7.

lawn. We were rotated around these jobs. The family worked together.⁶

This blest and happy childhood was Kay's most treasured memories:

> We were never molested, [or] frightened by anything . . . . We had an amazingly blessed childhood. Our parents never argued in front of us.⁷ We had enough and we were never aware of any lack. The more I hear about other people's upbringing, the more I realized how blessed I am - It was quite rare.⁸

When Kay was 13 years old, she attended a youth camp, where she accepted the Lord. However, she was not followed up or discipled. Everyone assumed that since she went to church regularly, she would be fine. Thus, her life transformation did not begin. She had no sense of a personal relationship with the Lord. She felt like she didn't need to bother God with any problems; she didn't expect Him to intervene either.⁹

Thus, salvation and a personal relationship with God was an enormous revelation to Kay even though she had been to church all her life.¹⁰ For her, Christianity meant obeying the rules. She was good at it and became extremely self-righteous.¹¹ She thought that God was a theory and didn't expect Him to answer. But one day, when she was having a major problem, she talked to God about it and was shocked to hear Him in an almost audible voice! She started reading books and talked to a Pentecostal friend to find out more about God.¹²

It was during her early twenties, while going through a failed engagement, that she read the book *Beyond Ourselves* by Catherine

---

⁶Ibid., 7.
⁷Ibid., 4.
⁸Ibid., 14.
⁹Ibid., 8.
¹⁰Ibid., 7.
¹¹Ibid., 3.
¹²Ibid., 7.

Marshall. She realized that she needed a personal relationship with God.[13] She described how God saved her from being self-righteous: "I didn't repent of my sins, when I got saved because I didn't think I was a sinner. It took a while for the Lord to show me I was a sinner. . . . I gave the Lord permission to take control of my life."[14]

This marked the beginning of a radical change in her life and understanding of Christianity.[15] Kay considered this as her spiritual birthday for a long time until one day when she went to check out a camp location for their high school class. As she walked on to the camp site, she remembered what happened when she was 13 years old at that same place. It was like the Lord gently whispered to her, "You forgot but I remembered."[16]

Kay experienced the baptism of the Holy Spirit while at home, alone, after reading the book *Nine O'clock in the Morning* by Dennis and Rita Bennett. She was still going to the Presbyterian Church where she had been brought up. But a few years later, she relocated from Wellington to Auckland and began to attend a Church of Christ. A couple from that church perceived that she was a Spirit-filled believer and alerted her that the pastor did not approve of such practice. They suggested that she go to a local Assembly of God church which became her home church for the next forty years.[17]

Kay enjoyed school as a whole and was always at the top of her class without exerting much effort. However, by the time she went on to college and was in high school and university, she was distracted and became less motivated.[18] Nonetheless, she graduated with honors with a Bachelor of Science major in Mathematics from Victoria University, in

---

[13]Ibid., 8.
[14]Ibid., 3.
[15]Ibid., 8.
[16]Ibid.
[17]Kay Fountain, email to author, 12 January 2016.
[18]Fountain interview, 6.

Wellington, New Zealand in 1973 and also earned a Diploma in Teaching at the New Zealand Education Department in 1974.[19]

Ministry Call

While at the height of her teaching career, the Lord spoke to her about an international teaching ministry. Several thoughts went through her mind: First, she told God, "You cannot have an international ministry when nobody knows who you are." She didn't realize yet that "if God knew who you were - it doesn't matter if nobody knew you." Second, she was not involved in any ministry, and argued, "God, I'm a high school teacher and an international teaching ministry does not apply to me." She thought God must have "accidentally dialed a wrong number."[20]

These thoughts were put back on the shelf because Kay did not consider herself a minister, although she was saved and baptized in the Holy Spirit. She desperately wanted to be a missionary. In fact, for many years she answered missionary altar calls, asking God to call her. Many years later she realized that God had indeed done so.[21]

Outstanding Student

Aside from being a high school mathematics teacher for several years in two different schools, Kay also worked at Takapuna Assembly of God (now Harbourside Church, in North Shore City, New Zealand) and was in charge of Adult Christian Education. She served as Instructor of ICI University for six years in her home country. In 1987, she wrote the

---

[19]"A. Kay Fountain," available at http:// www.apts.edu/indexcfm?menuid=72 &parentid=19 (accessed November 24, 2015).
[20]Fountain interview, 2.
[21]Ibid., 3.

Teacher's Guide for ICI Christian Service Program book, *Abundant Living: A Study of the Fruit of the Spirit*.[22]

Studying in Bible school and seminary were two of Kay's major decisions. She attended Zion Bible Training Centre in Auckland, New Zealand and graduated 1983 with a diploma. This was credited towards her B.A. in Bible and Theology from the International Correspondence Institute (ICI – now Global University)[23] where she graduated in 1986.[24] Dr. John Carter the Dean of the College of ICI then, mentioned her exceptional achievement:

> Kay was always an outstanding student. . . . She was selected by ICI's US accrediting association, the National Home Study Council, as the outstanding graduate among all the BA programs they accredited in the US and internationally. The award included a trip to Washington D.C. from her home in New Zealand to receive the honor in a ceremony at their headquarters. On her way, she stopped in Brussels to visit ICI. I was on a trip at that time, but Bea hosted her visit and reported on what a delightful woman she was.[25]

In 1993, Kay came to APTS with plans to teach Bible school in Africa after completing her M.A. in ministry. In her first term as a student, she earned a 4.0 grade point average and it dawned on her that she was actually capable of achieving high grades in an international setting. She took this as God's confirmation to stay for a M.Div. degree. Furthermore, Dr. John Carter, seeing her great academic potential encouraged her to consider a Ph. D. and an M. Div. was the way to start.[26] He described Kay's academic excellence in this manner: "Kay was always the best

---

[22]"A. Kay Fountain."
[23]Fountain, email to author, 12 January 2016.
[24]John Carter, email to author, 23 September 2015.
[25]Ibid.
[26]Fountain interview, 12-13.

student in my classes, where I would give her A+ grades because she exceeded the requirement for an A. Unfortunately, the APTS grade system did not provide for this to be recorded as her final course grade, so that was always an "A." Her overall academic record also reflected this level of achievement."[27]

Kay was thrilled to do an M.A. at APTS without having to write a thesis. But after graduating with an MA in Ministry with honors in 1994, she realized that in New Zealand, a master's degree without a thesis was not recognized.[28] Thus, she wrote *An Exploratory Study of Levels of Moral Reasoning among Filipino College Students as a Function of Academic Setting (Theological or Secular), Level of Self-Esteem and Gender*[29] as her M.Div. thesis and graduated with honors in 1995.[30]

President William Menzies recommended that Kay join the APTS Faculty in Training program after completing her M. Div. degree. At this point, God prompted Kay about her missionary call 17 years previously:[31]

> [After] Dr. Bill Menzies asked me to join the faculty, that's when the Lord reminded me, "I told you—you would be doing an international ministry." So it was . . . [that it] all came together. The call was already there and I only recognized it a lot later. . . . I didn't have this huge plan of what the Lord was going to do in my life. I was just kind [of thinking that] if God wants me to do something—I'll do it in single steps of obedience.[32]

---

[27] Carter email.
[28] Fountain interview, 13.
[29] "A. Kay Fountain."
[30] Fountain, 12 January 2016.
[31] Fountain interview, 2.
[32] Fountain, 13.

Missionary- Instructor and Administrator Serving at APTS

In 1995, Kay became an ordained minister with the New Zealand Assemblies of God and began to teach for APTS under missionary appointment the following year. She continued to excel as a student and completed her Ph.D. in the Old Testament at the University of Auckland in 1998 in less than three years.[33] Actually, "she had to delay submitting her dissertation to fulfill the time requirement."[34] Wonsuk Ma, the academic dean of APTS at that time, considered Kay's addition to the faculty as a significant event for two reasons: "First, she strengthened the Old Testament studies instantaneously. . . . Second, her Old Testament study was uniquely shaped to bring a contemporary response to the ancient text. This was an important angle as the old texts should be made relevant to today's believers."[35]

As faculty, Kay has extended her teaching expertise and influence outside the Baguio campus through APTS extension classes to other places in the Philippines and several countries of the Asia Pacific region including Mongolia, Australia and New Zealand.[36]

APTS Students know Kay as a brilliant Old Testament professor and a caring disciplinarian.[37] They all agreed that she is firm and required students to follow the syllabus, come to class and submit requirements on time.[38] An Asian student commented that it was a "good discipline for Asians to manage our time."[39] When students plagiarized she was always disappointed.[40] She set a good example by never being late to her classes except for emergencies.[41] Kay "approached her work with such

---

[33]Carter email.
[34]Ibid.
[35]Wonsuk Ma, email to author, 24 September, 2015.
[36]Carolyn Tejedo, email to author, 16 November, 2015.
[37]Joel Tejedo, interview by Dynnice Rosanny Engcoy, 11 October, 2015, Baguio City, Philippines.
[38]Tejedo interview, 1; Wang Hang (Bettina), email to author, 23 November, 2015.
[39]Hang email.
[40]Fountain, 25 November, 2015.
[41]Hang email.

efficiency that she marked and returned essays in record time."[42] Yet, she cared for her students by sharing with, praying for, and helping them academically and spiritually. Bettina, who currently teaches in a Bible school in Southwest China, also felt cared for by Kay. She explained how honored she was to be Kay's student and explained that Kay not only taught biblical knowledge, but also cared for her students by encouraging them in their intimacy with Christ. Kay impacted Bettina's life in particular one day when she told her, "You can complain to God, because He is your Father, and He loves you."[43] This experience encouraged her to finish her study at APTS and begin ministry in China.

Joel Tejedo, another former student and now a faculty member at APTS recalled another incident of Kay's caring. When his wife had a miscarriage, Kay visited them and became their friend and pastor inside the campus.[44] She "looked for opportunities to be an encourager and a role model for the students and was willing to pray through crises."[45]

Kay's caring attitude extended to her home. Students who needed a place to stay found Kay's home a haven. Several of them have benefited from her "sound wisdom and advice" through "deep, honest, heart to heart conversation."[46] They were privileged to watch her spirituality up close. Enkhee, a student from Mongolia, saw her love and devotion to "study God's word in Hebrew and Greek" and it never failed to amaze her.[47] Denise, one of her roommates also observed that

> Dr. Kay was deeply committed to God and she started the morning routine with her Greek and Hebrew Bible out on her balcony overlooking the valley. She often related some new revelations excitedly. She asked God to speak to her about a

---

[42]Denise Ross, email to author, 14 October 2015.
[43]Hang email.
[44]Tejedo interview, 1.
[45]Ross email.
[46]Ibid.
[47]Enkhbayar Batsuren, email to author, 18 January 2016.

situation, whether it would be making a decision, solving a conflict or relating to her leisure activities.[48]

Not only did Kay bless others, she was also richly blessed by living in a multicultural environment of APTS. She commented that unless one lived with other cultures, believers "will not understand how much of their interpretation of the Bible is culturally conditioned." She recalled her cross-cultural encounter:

> When I first came to APTS, I thought all my theology was correct and everybody must agree with me. Then, I started realizing that people didn't agree with me not because they were not Christians, but because they came from a different culture. It's the cultural understanding of things—my eyes were opened. . . . The richness of cross-cultural Bible study is that you get a deeper understanding than you would have, if you stayed in your own culture—because it deepens with what other cultures bring to the table.[49]

Kay serves with distinction as faculty and an administrator. She has administered post-graduate programs as the Associate Academic Dean of the Center for Asian Pentecostal Studies for several years and was appointed as APTS' Academic Dean in 2012.[50] Kay worked hard and provided "excellent oversight to the development and administration of the APTS faculty and academic programs."[51] Being an Academic Dean, one has to take a "pastoral role for a multicultural"[52] academic team and keep them "functioning efficiently and harmoniously."[53] Wonsuk Ma gave an insight as to how the APTS Dean played that role:

---

[48]Ross email.
[49]Fountain interview, 15.
[50]Carter email; Fountain, 12 January 2016.
[51]Carter email.
[52]Ma email.
[53]Ibid.

Just like a parish minister, who lives in the community, [the] Dean's job at APTS was a 24/7 one. I am sure this applies to her as well. For this, she deserved a standing ovation and this festschrift is a fitting one. I know this challenging job was her conscious decision as it was for me. I once told someone: "The President shapes the body of the seminary, the Dean shapes its soul."[54]

Mountain Ministries

Ministry for Kay is not only confined in the classroom; she is also actively involved in different ministries in the local church, in nearby communities, and beyond.[55] She ministered in remote churches in the surrounding regions sometimes staying with local people. Many times she rode on jeepneys, trucks and buses before she owned her own vehicle.[56] Ma commented on these trips:

> Her dusty truck was a sure testimony to her deep commitment to the careful study of the Bible in order to nurture Christian life and vocation. Her Kiwi spirit must have bred this creative edge refusing to be limited by established paradigms or boundaries. APTS must have been immensely blessed by this "spirited" dean.[57]

Teaching and Ministerial Role: Mongolia AG

Kay's first trip to Mongolia was in 1995, while doing a Field Education requirement for her M. Div. She spent ten weeks teaching in a Bible school, teaching English and ministering at the church. Since

---

[54]Ibid.
[55]Lou Gomez, email to author, 30 October 2015.
[56]Ross email.
[57]Ma email.

then, Kay has made this mission trip of teaching and preaching among local churches annually, except for the years 2011-13.[58] She served as an advisor to the National Council of the Assemblies of God in Mongolia[59] and accepted the responsibility as an interim Senior Pastor of Hope Church in 2000-01. It was the first and the largest Assemblies of God church in Mongolia.[60] Rev. Kem Price, one of Kay's mentors and former Overseas Mission Director of New Zealand Assemblies of God mentioned that this decision was crucial, because "key leaders were emerging from the Bible College in Mongolia that needed more consistent mentoring and development."[61] Enkhee and Bayaraa, who served Hope Church for more than twenty years, expressed how Kay assisted them through a transition:

> Hope Church was going through transition, from being a church supported by the American Assemblies of God . . . [to] a more independent, indigenous church. Pastor Bob has started that vision, but it was Dr. Kay who has pushed us to have more faith in God . . . . We have moved from 40 to 100 percent indepeden[ce] financially.[62]

The congregation in Mongolia acknowledged that Kay is a strong leader that will not back down when enemies come.[63] She has a "tenacity and fearlessness to take on challenges"[64] and does things based on the word of God and "not according to worldly standards."[65] She was firm and lives by the principles she teaches.[66]

---

[58] Batsuren email; Fountain, 12 January 2016.
[59] "A. Kay Fountain."
[60] Kem Price, email to author, 14 January 2016, New Zealand; Fountain, 12 January 2016; Batsuren email.
[61] Ibid.
[62] Batsuren email.
[63] Ibid.
[64] Price email.
[65] Batsuren email.
[66] Ibid.

Senior Pastor at International Praise Center (IPC)

Kay has never sought for any position but takes responsibility for whatever the Lord has given her.[67] She first served IPC as Missions Pastor in 2005 and two years later, she became the Senior Pastor until February, 2018.[68]

One of Kay's major gifts is being an encourager.[69] She "loves investing in both potential and current leaders."[70] She encourages members to be actively involved in ministry and missions by her example.[71] When they do, she is quick to affirm. Joel Abadayan, IPC treasurer reminisced, "one time she asked me to share and speak at church about giving. She affirmed me and I was greatly encouraged that God can use me." Kay also led a team from the church to go for missions trips in Ilocos province[72] and those that went had the opportunity to be involved as worship and Bible study leaders.[73] Judah Sumcad, Worship Director at IPC, said that when he was struggling and was about to give up the ministry, Kay counselled him to stay on.[74]

Kay has cared deeply for the wellbeing of the IPC leadership team and the whole congregation. An old-timer from IPC said, "[Pastor] Kay loves and cares for me [in ways] that I have not seen from others."[75]

---

[67]Ibid.
[68]Fountain, 12 January 2016.
[69]Fountain, 25 November 2015.
[70]Price email.
[71]Remedios Bautista, interview by Dynnice Rosanny Engcoy, 11 October, 2015, Baguio City, Philippines.
[72]Annabelle de Borja, interview by Dynnice Rosanny Engcoy, 11 October, 2015, Baguio City, Philippines; Anna Cristiana Antolin, interview by Dynnice Rosanny Engcoy, 11 October, 2015, Baguio City, Philippines.
[73]De Borja interview, 1.
[74]Judah Sumcad, interview by Dynnice Rosanny Engcoy, 11 October, 2015, Baguio City, Philippines.
[75]Trifonia E. Miana, interview by Dynnice Rosanny Engcoy, 11 October, 2015, Baguio City, Philippines.

Along with her gift of encouragement, IPC church members treasured Kay's passion to teach and preach the word.[76] She presented Scriptures in simple terms.[77] Enkhee also testified to this:

> I admired her ability to take something deep and make it so simple enough that a child can understand and also taking something simple and mak[ing] it so deep. I like the way she answers questions, always going back to the Bible and giving biblical reasons, and sharing her testimony to make the point clear.[78]

IPC was blest by her extensive knowledge of the word of God and sound theology which were evident in her teaching and preaching.[79] Joel Abadayan remarked, "I grew spiritually because I learned many things from her."[80] Joseph Antolin, a youth worker also said, "I always look forward to her preaching."[81] Kay is focused when she sets objectives, but in the midst of her planning, "she leaves room for the Holy Spirit to work in her life." [82]

In the course of Kay's ministerial role at IPC, the church recognized her "objective way of dealing with people."[83] She is open to suggestions and "listens to everybody's opinion but knows when to intervene and give her wise counsel."[84] She is "tough but also gentle. She knows how to confront people without damaging their soul. She is firm on disciplining people, correcting wrong doings and [is] compassionate."[85] She never

---

[76]Ibid.
[77]Tavita Pagaialii, email to author, 24 September 2015, Samoa; Belina Gaiwen, interview by Dynnice Rosanny Engcoy, 11 October, 2015, Baguio City, Philippines.
[78]Batsuren email.
[79]Sumcad interview, 1
[80]Joel Abadayan, interview by Dynnice Rossany Engcoy, 11 October, 2015, Baguio City, Philippines.
[81]Antolin, A. interview, 1.
[82]De Borja interview, 1.
[83]Gaiwen interview, 1.
[84]Sumcad interview, 1; Antolin, A. interview, 1.
[85]Batsuren email.

stopped caring for her parishioners even those who opposed her[86] and she "handles hard situations in a peaceful manner."[87] Denise observed: "Any conflict weighed heavily on her heart and after seeking God's will, she set out to put things straight. She talked to people honestly and fairly while preserving their dignity. Both her integrity and love were evident."[88]

Concluding Memories

Even though she has no family of her own, Kay regards Racquel, her house helper, as well as the whole IPC church as her own family. In this family she also includes starving and dying kittens that she nourished to health at her home! Racquel fondly expressed that it was a joy to work at Kay's home, ". . . [S]he always reminds all the students that lived with her to treat me as part of her family. I considered her not only as my boss, but a mom, sister and a friend. . . . She has been good, loving, thoughtful and understanding to me."[89]

While her ministries have crossed national boundaries and have been intense and varied, Kay's life verse, Matthew 6:33,[90] helped her seek a balanced approach to life and ministry. Those who know Kay recognized that she was and is an outstanding theological educator, a passionate missionary, and a devoted pastor who remarkably balances and fulfills the demands of leadership roles both at the seminary and the church efficiently.[91] And yet, she still has time for fun and leisure. These qualities are rarely found in one person.[92]

This balance in Kay's approach to life includes a love for fun and adventure which started when Kay was young. She loved snow skiing,

---

[86]Tejedo interview, 1; Gaiwen interview, 1.
[87]Antolin A, 1.
[88]Ross email.
[89]Raquel Dado, email to author, 11 November, 2015, Baguio City, Philippines.
[90]Fountain, 25 November, 2015.
[91]Carter email; Tejedo interview, 1; Ma email; Price email.
[92]Carter email.

was a sprinter, and a provincial field hockey representative in her high school and university years. She also played the piano and violin.[93] She broadened her horizons for fun and adventure even further when she became a divemaster and eventually a scuba dive instructor.[94] She felt this would give her opportunity to link with another segment of the community and increase the diversity of her ministry in the Philippines.[95]

A young person from IPC said, "She is fond of outdoor trips" and "a fun person to be with."[96] She often takes students for a trip to the Hundred Islands, one of the tourist destinations in the Philippines. Everyone always looks forward to a time of fun, food, and fellowship with her.[97] A student remarked, "It was so relaxing and encouraging for all of us who went."[98]

Kay Fountain is a highly respected minister and servant of God. Those whose lives she touched cherish her as their friend, colleague, teacher, preacher, pastor, mother, sister, spiritual mentor, a positive role model and a beloved family member. While she has strengths and weaknesses just like anybody else, through it all, she has kept her faith and Spirit—awareness up front. In her own words: "Everything God has done in my life is so amazing—who am I now, the whole journey—is God's success story."[99]

---

[93] Fountain interview, 4.
[94] Ross email; Price email.
[95] Price email.
[96] Juvy Ann Vicente, interview by Dynnice Rosanny Engcoy, 11 October 2015, Baguio City, Philippines.
[97] Ross email; Tejedo interview 1.
[98] Tejedo interview, 1.
[99] Fountain interview, 12.

Bibliography

Abadayan, Joel. Interview by Dynnice Rosanny Engcoy, 11 October 2015, Baguio City, Philippines.

"A. Kay Fountain," available at http://www.apts.edu/indexcfm?menuid =72&parentid=19 (accessed November 24, 2015).

Batsuren, Enkhbayar. Email to author, 18 January 2016.

Bautista, Remedios. Interview by Dynnice Rosanny Engcoy, 11 October 2015, Baguio City, Phillippines.

Borja de, Annabelle. Interview by Dynnice Rosanny, 11 October 2015, Baguio City, Philippines.

Carter, John. Email to author, 23 September 2015.

Duncan, Trish. Email to author, 22 January 2016.

Dado, Racquel. Email to author, 11 November 2015.

Fountain, Kay. Email to author, 25 November 2015.

_____. Email to author, 12 January 2016.

Gaiwen, Belina. Interview by Dynnice Rosanny Engcoy, 11 October 2015, Baguio City, Philippines.

Gomez, Lou. Email to author, 30 October 2015.

Hang, Wang. Email to author, 23 November 2015.

Ma, Wonsuk. Email to author, 24 September 2015.

Miana, Trifonia. Interview by Dynnice Rosanny Engcoy, 11 October 2015, Baguio City, Philippines.

Pagaialiii, Tavita. Email to author, 24 September 2015.

Price, Kem. Email to author, 14 January 2016.

Ross, Denise. Email to author, 14 October 2015.

Sumcad, Judah. Interview by Dynnice Rosanny Engcoy, 11 October 2015, Baguio City, Philippines.

Tejedo, Carolyn. Email to author, 18 November 2015.

Tejedo, Joel. Interview by Dynnice Rosanny Engcoy, 11 October 2015, Baguio City, Philippines.

Vicente, Judy Ann. Interview by Dynnice Rosanny Engcoy, 11 October 2015, Baguio City, Philippines.

ASIAN THEOLOGICAL EDUCATION: *NOW AND THEN*
AN ASIAN PENTECOSTAL PASTOR-EDUCATOR'S SURVEY OF THEOLOGICAL EDUCATION

by Tham Wan Yee

Introduction

This paper is an attempt to describe some of the issues around the debate on theological education and set the Asian Pentecostal theological education enterprise against that background. I will conclude with some personal thoughts on the future of Pentecostal theological education in Asia.

Let me start by describing my own personal journey in theological education. After my conversion at age 13, I was immediately discipled by my church using material from the Navigators and Campus Crusade for Christ. I was taught the disciplines of the evangelical Christian life, like "daily quiet time" that includes prayer and Bible reading, "witnessing," regular group Bible studies, systematic Scripture memory, etc. As I grew spiritually in church, I was also encouraged to take up night classes at the Bible Institute of Malaysia (which later became the Bible College of Malaysia[1] or BCM). I started the night classes in 1976, while I was in the first year of my pre-university studies. Those first classes were taught by missionaries from the United States Assemblies of God missions department. The BCM classes were different from my pre-university

---

[1]For more information about the Bible College of Malaysia, please visit www.bcm.org.my/.

studies, in course content as well as in course structure (including both delivery styles and course requirements). My pre-university studies were structured along the British education system while BCM followed the American education system.

The British and American education systems are very different because they have different underlying philosophies. Some have suggested that in the British system, every student starts with zero and has to earn their points; while in the American system, every student starts with 100 points, which is theirs to lose. The British education system assumes that people have different abilities and attempts to differentiate people into different classes, while the American education system starts by assuming that all are equal and tries to pull everyone up to a higher class. Another big difference I noticed at that time was that in the American education system, course assignments contributed to the final grade of the student, while the British system's grading depended almost totally on the results of the student's performance in examinations.

After working as an accountant and owning my own business for a while, I was invited to be the full-time pastor for my home church. It was then that I started studying full-time at BCM. (Although I was a full-time student at BCM, I was not a residential student because there were no facilities for married students at BCM at that time.) I went on to graduate with a B.Th. in 1989—almost 13 years after my first night classes there. During the final year of my B.Th. studies, I started studying with the Far East Advanced School of Theology (FEAST) through its extension program in Malaysia. FEAST was at that time transitioning into becoming a graduate seminary: the Asia Pacific Theological Seminary (APTS).[2] The extension program was run in three-week intensive blocks, with most of the students being full-time pastors.

In 1996, I received a note from the APTS Registrar informing me that I would lose all the credits I had gained from my studies with APTS

---

[2]Asia Pacific Theological Seminary, www.apts.edu.

if I did not complete my M.A. in Ministry by a certain date. By then, I had pastored for more than 10 years and felt it would be the right time to take a "sabbatical." I initially studied full-time for one trimester (3 months) at APTS' main campus in Baguio, Philippines and finished with my M.A. in Ministry. I enjoyed it so much that I returned immediately to study for another trimester, this time with my whole family (wife and 3 sons). After that, I continued with some more courses in the Malaysian extension program. The APTS Dean at that time, Wonsuk Ma, then encouraged me to consider the possibility of continuing my studies in the new post-graduate Th.M. program that APTS was planning to start in 2000. Having enjoyed my theological education so far, and seeing that the structure of the new Th.M. program would not require me to leave my pastoral ministry, I agreed to join the first cohort of the APTS Master of Theology program. I graduated in 2004 with my Th.M. in Pentecostal and Charismatic Studies.

It was while still studying for my Th.M. that Ma invited me to join APTS as a missionary-faculty. I taught part-time at BCM while I also served as the part-time Business Administrator. I was therefore already very involved in theological education, even while pastoring full-time. I resigned from my pastoral position in 2002 and joined the Malaysian Assembly of God (AG) World Missions Department (WMD) as a missionary candidate. After itinerating for 2 years, I became a full-time faculty at APTS (almost immediately after I graduated with my Th.M.). As in many Asian seminary settings, as a full-time faculty, I had to serve in administrative roles in the school while managing a full teaching load. On top of this, my wife and I pioneered a church on the weekends. This, I must stress, is quite common for Asians serving as Bible school professors. The "weekend ministry" is often an opportunity to model ministry to students.

After over 5 years of full-time involvement at APTS, I was asked to be the President of the seminary. It was quite an honor but also a daunting prospect. After prayer and consultation with my sending agency, my wife and I decided that I should take the challenge. In 2009, I became the first President of APTS in its 45-year history to come from outside of the American Assemblies of God.

My personal journey in theological education has not been very intentional but it has allowed me, perhaps, to experience it at different levels and to see it from different angles. I started my theological studies as a part-time, night class student, studying as a lay church member. Then, I went into full-time theological studies, while pastoring a church on the weekends. After graduating from a local Bible college, I went into graduate and post-graduate studies in an international seminary. I then went on to become a seminary professor and administrator. More recently, I have been given the privilege of leading one of the most influential seminaries in the region.

While I have been privileged to study and work at different levels of the theological education enterprise, I should perhaps add that my views here will be limited (and perhaps even biased) by the fact that I have been involved only in a Pentecostal setting. While working on this paper, I have tried to read as much as I can on the subject so that I can have a wider background from which to present my views. I also need to understand the issues involved in the conversation out there and the language being used. Even then, I need to confess that I am not formally trained as an educator, neither am I a "pure academician." I am more of a pastor who believes in the value of theological education.

Definitions & Delimitations

Where and What is Asia?

As we talk about Asian theological education, we need to ask where and what is Asia? The multitude of cultures and vast variety of ethnic groups that comprise Asia makes it very difficult to define. It includes more than 50 countries/territories from Taiwan to Turkey, and from Siberia to Singapore. The 2002 Busan Asian Games, which followed the break-up of the Soviet Union (and therefore included countries from the former Soviet Union states of Central Asia), had participants of every skin color of the human race: yellow, brown, black and white. Asia is very pluralistic—certainly not monolithic.

In a pointed article in the February 12, 1987 issue of the *Far Eastern Economic Review*, Philip Bowring asked the question: "What is 'Asia'?"[3] He suggested in the article that the delimitation of what is considered Asia today does not really follow natural geography and the identity of Asia was really a convenient label given by the colonial masters of Europe. He further suggested that the continuing identity of Asia is a reaction to European actions and attitudes. Therefore, Asia's identity is found in its history rather than its geography.

With reference to the theological enterprise, "Asia" is often limited to East and South Asia. Because of its inclusion in the Soviet Union, much of Central Asia has been out of the Asian loop, so to say, for much of its modern history. West Asia (including Iran and the so-called Middle East), despite its influence in earlier years of church history, is usually not considered under the subject of Asian Theology. Instead, it is often considered under the rubric of "Islamic Studies" in mission circles today.

For the same reasons Asian theology is necessary, it is also important to consider Asian theological education in its local contexts. It does not mean a parochial or anti-West approach to learning. Asian theological educators must appreciate not just the uniqueness of Asia but the global potential of Asia as well. The famous Critical Asian Principle proposed by Emerito Nacpil in the seventies continues to have currency and was recently brought back to the discussion table.[4] While Asia may have changed, the ideals of the Critical Asian Principle remain. They are: (1) to promote an Asian orientation in theological education in the Southeast Asian region and (2) to seek and identify what is "distinctly

---

[3]Philip Browning, "What is 'Asia'?," Colombia University, http://afe.easia.columbia.edu/ geography/geo_whatis.html (accessed 27th May 2015).
[4]*International Bulletin of Missionary Research* 32.2 (Apr 2008): 77-80.

Asian and use such distinctiveness as a critical principle of judgment on matters dealing with the life and mission of the Christian community, theology, and theological education in Asia."[5]

What is THEOLOGICAL Education?

What makes theological education *theological*? While the content or curriculum is important, it is probably more than just a matter of the curriculum. Whether formal, non-formal, or informal,[6] theological education (like all forms of good education) is to inform as well as to form individuals. The "information" and "formation" processes have more than just private and personal impact. The process leads to conformation and transformation of the individual being educated, as well as the people and the environment that the individual has influence over. The words, "conform" and "transform" are borrowed from Rom. 12:1-2 and deliberately used here to reflect similar meanings as they are used in that biblical text. Pentecostals may prefer to use more dramatic words like "impact" and "impartation." As we are talking about Christian theological education, this process can involve education at every level (from Sunday School to Adult Bible Class to full-time ministerial training) in the Church and the academy.

There is theological education outside of the local church and seminary setting too. After I became a full-time pastor, I began to realize that there were many seminars available that were specifically designed to appeal to pastors, and that I could continue to educate and equip myself with well-chosen seminars. I suspect that this might be one of the reasons why some pastors without a background in formal Bible

---

[5]Ibid.

[6]A helpful set of definitions for "formal (school education)," "non-formal (non-school education, but dependent and controlled by official education)," and "informal (autonomous in relation to the official education system and imparted by extra-scholastic groups or institutions)" is found in Washington Padilla, "Non-Formal Theological Education" in *New Alternatives in Theological Education*, ed. C. Rene Padilla and tr. Patricia Mae Crowley (Oxford, London: Regnum Books, 1988): 97-139, 100.

school/seminary would still feel that they can be sufficiently well-equipped for the ministry. Seminars are often more practical and contemporary than seminaries. But, can a regime of well-chosen seminars actually replace seminary learning? One major consideration is that while we can choose our regime of seminars, our choices tend to be affected by our biases. We will avoid some areas of learning and this may lead to weaknesses and blind spots in our personal ministry and spiritual formation. Seminaries, on the other hand, will have prerequisites and core courses so that foundational areas are covered to ensure more holistic learning. Seminary education also forces a student into different modes of learning when they sit under different professors of varying teaching styles. Ministry or pastoral seminars can provide non-formal education to add to a formal Bible school/seminary education.

For this paper, the term "theological education" will refer to the whole enterprise of intentionally developing workers for the ministry. While some may hesitate to use the word "professional" to describe the ministry, the specific scope of this paper has to do with the training of full-time, career[7] workers for the ministry; i.e. ministerial training.

So, we now have the background, context and scope of this paper. I want to emphasize again that this paper expresses my *personal* views on the current and future situations of Pentecostal-Evangelical theological education in Asia (especially in East and Southeast Asia). These personal views have not come from a vacuum. My own life has been impacted by theological education. While theological education can cover the whole range of Christian education, the main thrust of this paper has to do with formal ministerial training.

---

[7] It is interesting to see how both the words, "curriculum" and "career" are so similar in meaning when we consider their etymologies. Both suggest the idea of a "race course." Online Etymology Dictionary. http://www.etymonline.com/ (accessed 1st June 2015).

Brief Survey of The Models of Theological Education

Historical Models

In reviewing the history of theological education in general (and not just limited to professional ministerial training), Sidney Rooy describes four historical models:[8]

1. The **catechetical model**, which was used in the first two centuries of the Church, with its emphasis on pastoral concerns and discipleship;
2. The **monastic model**, which developed from the 2nd century up to the beginning of the Middle Ages, with its emphasis on separation and private spirituality;
3. The **scholastic model**, which flourished in the Middle Ages with an emphasis on the academic development of the clergy; and,
4. The **seminary model**, which developed after the Reformation and has persisted until today, with an emphasis on a well-rounded "professional" training for the clergy.

Rooy suggests that all the theological education models in church history are still being used in some ways today. The catechetical model is now seen in what is often called "Christian Education" in local churches, while the monastic model is still found in some closed ecclesiastical communities. The scholastic model may have been rejected by the Protestant church immediately after the Reformation but it came back later as closed doctrinal systems took root in some Protestant denominations. The seminary model is the ubiquitous model for professional ministerial training today. While these models may be different from each other, Rooy claims that all of them have an elitist

---

[8]Sidney Rooy, "Historical Models of Theological Education," in *New Alternatives in Theological Education*, (Oxford: Regnum, 1988),51-72.

dominance, with those at the top dominating the process and "serve to maintain and strengthen ecclesiastical society itself."[9] He therefore calls on God's people (the *laos*) to consider the strengths of these models, and also to move beyond all these models, to construct a new model that will respond to a changing world.

Limiting his overview to the United States, Edward Farley suggests two ways to periodize the history of theological education there. One is to look at it in terms of the *location* of the training of ministers, and see two historical periods: "pre-seminary and seminary." Another is to look at it in terms of the *nature of the education*, allowing for three periods: "the period of pious learning (divinity), the period of specialized learning, and the period of professional learning." He further suggests that the first period of "pious learning" coincides roughly with the "pre-seminary period."[10] Farley was commenting from the perspective of the late 1980's on the American situation. It may be good for us to ask today if we have already entered a "post-seminary" period of theological education. Following up on Rooy's call for a new model, we, as God's people, might want to have input into the development of a new post-seminary model.

Philosophical Models

David Kelsey suggests that we use two models of education (which he labels as "Athens" and "Berlin") to consider what theological education entails.[11] The Athens model follows the Greek *paideia* philosophy of education, which assumes a given "Ultimate Good" that students are to be taught to follow. The Berlin model is a university model and a research model, which encourage critical questioning and learning. Kelsey sees these two models as "normative" and yet

---

[9]Ibid., 69.
[10]Edward Farley, *Theologia: The Fragmentation and Unity of Theological Education* (Philadelphia: Fortress Press, 1983), 6ff.
[11]David H. Kelsey, *Between Athens and Berlin: The Theological Education Debate* (Grand Rapids: Eerdmans, 1993), n.p.

"contrasting" and "finally irreconcilable." He, however, hinted at the possibility of a third model with its roots in Jerusalem that might provide the resolution.[12]

Robert Banks took that cue and added a "Jerusalem" model into the mix of theological education models.[13] Banks' model is a missional model, which he took care to explain, is more than just a missiological emphasis. He suggests *missiologia* (contra Farley's *theologia*[14] and Stackhouse's *apologia*[15]) as the integrative factor giving coherence to theological education. Banks cites Kaehler's dictum, that mission is "the mother of theology" to support his grounding of theological education in mission. For Banks, "mission stimulates theological education" and "theological education is a dimension of mission."[16]

Brian Edgar further muddled the picture by throwing in yet another model, which he labeled as the "Geneva" model.[17] The Geneva "confessional" model Edgar proposed is perhaps a throwback to the scholastic model.

So, now the original Athens-Berlin tension has developed into a multi-model matrix of four different theological education philosophies. Willem de Wit tries to bring some clarity into the whole with his helpful presentation on the next page (Figure 1):[18]

---

[12] Ibid., 5.

[13] Robert Banks, *Reenvisioning Theological Education: Exploring a Missional Alternative to Current Models* (Grand Rapids: Eerdmans, 1999), 127.

[14] Farley, *Theologia: The Fragmentation and Unity of Theological Education*, np.

[15] Max L. Stackhouse, *Apologia: Contextualization, Globalization and Mission in Education* (Grand Rapids: Eerdmans, 1988), n.p.

[16] Banks, 131. Banks is here citing largely from an article by Orlando E. Costas, "Theological Education and Mission," in *New Alternatives in Theological Education*, 4-24.

[17] Brian Edgar, "The Theology of Theological Education," http://brian-edgar.com/wp-content/uploads/downloads/2010/05/Theology_of_Theological_Education.pdf (accessed 25th May 2015), 4.

[18] Williem-Jan de Wit, "Theology of Theological Education," http://willwmjdewit.com/2013/08/03/ theology-of-theological-education-the-athens-berlin-geneva-and-jerusalem-models/ (accessed 25th May 2015).

CLASSICAL	Transforming the individual	Knowing God	**CONFESSIONAL**
	ATHENS Academy	**GENEVA** Academy	
	THEOLOGIA MISSIOLOGY	DOXOLOGY SCIENTIA	
	ATHENS Academy	**BERLIN** University	
MISSIONAL	Converting the world	Strengthening the church	**VOCATIONAL**

Figure 1: Four Philosophical Models of Theological Education

A Teleological[19] Model: The Search for a Unifying Goal

Examples of the Goal from Different Traditions

One way to move away from the confusion of these competing models is to focus on the objective of the theological education enterprise. We have been presented with opposing good/viable options but these need not be either/or choices. We can embrace the whole or parts of the various options, as long as we remain focused on our goals for theological education in the context of Asia, which is to raise up Asian ministerial workers to fulfill the mission of God. In this respect, it is probably closer to Banks' missional Jerusalem model. This proposed teleological model is also similar to "proleptic pedagogy"[20] where theological education is done with an anticipation of the future. Proleptic

---

[19] The Greek word for "goal," *telos* is also the word for "maturity" or "perfection." Col. 1:28.

[20] Sondra Higgins Matthaei and Nancy R. Howell, *Proleptic Pedagogy: Theological Education Anticipating the Future* (Eugene, OR: Wipf and Stock, 2014), n.p.

pedagogy is not only teaching towards the future but teaching from the future as well. In Pentecostal circles, this might well be described as "prophetic pedagogy." Theological education in a rapidly changing world needs to anticipate the future and act as if the future is already here.

In a cursory survey of the literature on theological education, it is quite surprising to see how little emphasis is given to the goal of theological education, and how the goal should affect our model of theological education. Daniel Hardy says:

> Theological education needs a clear conception of its distinctive thrust—its goal. . . . The *goal*, I think, is an inhabited Wisdom (immersed in Scripture, the continuity of the Church's life in God, and in a Spirit-informed reason) in the Church, one that is active in responding to the issues of present day life.[21]

The Council of Trent was unapologetic and straightforward about the subservient role of theological education and defined the purpose of seminaries as "to train people loyal to the ideal of their Church, standing firm in the midst of the storm, with seriousness of purpose, absolute obedience, completely committed to the decisions of the Church."[22] Schleiermacher describes a somewhat similar purpose for theological education as "to bring forth true 'virtuosos of religion,' who will also be the 'princes of the Church' for modern times."[23] A more palatable word today for Schleiermacher's "princes" would be the word "leaders."

Costas was probably thinking of servant-leaders instead of just mere leaders or "princes" when he described the goal of theological education as "to form for the service of the Kingdom." Costas subdivided this into

---

[21] Daniel Hardy, cited by the "Hind Report" http://www.churchofengland.org/media/.../The%20Hind%20 report.doc (accessed 25th May 2015).
[22] Rooy, 68.
[23] F. D. Schleiermacher, cited by Rooy, 69.

three additional goals: "(1) the cultivating of love for God and neighbor, (2) training in order to articulate the faith precisely and contextually, and (3) development of the gift of discernment of the times for faithful obedience to the Kingdom."[24]

Henri Nouwen, noted Roman Catholic devotional theologian, and a strong advocate of spiritual formation as the goal of theological education, has this critique of theological education:

> What else is the goal of theological education than to bring us closer to the Lord our God so that we may be more faithful to the great commandment to love him with all our heart, with all our soul, and with all our mind, and our neighbor as ourselves (Matthew 22:37)? Seminaries and divinity schools must lead theology students into an ever-growing communion with God, with each other, and with their fellow human beings. Theological education is meant to form our whole person toward an increasing conformity with the mind of Christ so that our way of praying and our way of believing will be one.
> But is this what takes place? Often it seems that we who study or teach theology find ourselves entangled in such a complex network of discussions, debates, and arguments about God and "God-issues" that a simple conversation with God or a simple presence of God has become practically impossible...
> There was a time when the obvious milieu for theological education was the monastery. There words were born out of silence and could lead one deeper into silence. Although monasteries are no longer the most common places of theological education, silence remains as indispensable today as it was in the past. The Word of God is born out of the

---

[24]Costas, 22.

eternal silence of God, and it is to this Word out of silence that we want to be witnesses.[25]

Hardy (Anglican from the UK), Scheleirmacher (Liberal from 19th Century Germany), Costas (Evangelical from South America) and Nouwen (Roman Catholic from the US) were speaking from their own contexts and traditions. What about theological education in Asian Pentecostal circles? What do Asian Pentecostal educators hope to accomplish? It is very easy to be swept along by the routines of seminary activities and lose sight of the goal, especially in a well-established institution with long-standing policies and protocols for doing things. Pentecostalism in Asia is still relatively youthful and its theological education institutions have not yet been fossilized into unchanging monuments of the past. While institutions still have the ability to change, they need to be constantly reminded of their goal. The goal of an institution is the reason for its original foundation and continuing existence. It is the *pull* from the future and the *push* from the past. The focus on a unifying goal keeps theological education vibrant and dynamic in the present.

Since we have delimited our discussion for theological education on ministerial training, our goal for theological education in this context will have to do with the kind of ministers we are looking for. In the case of Pentecostals, the ideal minister is the one described as being "anointed." The goal for Pentecostal theological education will therefore be to produce anointed ministers for the Church. The concept of "anointing" is a very precious part of Pentecostal/Charismatic spirituality and comes from the Greek *Christos* and Hebrew *Mashiach*, which are transliterated into the English "Christ" and "Messiah."

---

[25]Henri Nouwen, *The Way of the Heart: Desert Spirituality and Contemporary Ministry* (New York: Harper Collins, 1991), 47-48.

Three anointed offices made up the national leadership structure of ancient Israel: Prophet, Priest and King. These were the ministers of the people of God in the Old Testament. Each of them played distinct roles and there was a separation of powers. But, as each of these offices failed at various times in Israel's history, people began to look forward to a heavenly messianic figure. Jesus is that heavenly Christ/Messiah which the people of Israel had been hoping for. He is THE Anointed One because now in one person resides all the three anointed offices of Prophet, Priest and King. An anointed minister has Jesus as his perfect model. The goal of theological education is to produce ministers after the example of Jesus.

Accreditation Standards: Compromised Goal?

Today, accrediting agencies/associations play an important role as guardians of the standards of excellence in theological education. There are currently three major accrediting associations representing different branches of the Protestant Church family. The Association for Theological Education in South East Asia (ATESEA) represents the liberal/ecumenical branch, the Asian Theological Association (ATA) represents the evangelical branch, while the Asia Pacific Theological Association (APTA) represents the Pentecostal/Charismatic branch. These associations are usually led by representatives of the larger institutions, thus reinforcing Rooy's complaint that theological education—whatever the model may be—is dominated by those at the top. Lest we become overly critical of the accreditation process, we need to recognize that these agencies play an important role and that most times, accredited schools or schools being evaluated for accreditation are already full-fledged members of these associations and are responsible for the directions these associations take. These associations not only serve as "enforcement" agencies to maintain the standards of excellence; they also serve as "empowerment" agencies, providing the training and network for mutual encouragement to help member schools meet the standards of excellence.

Robert Ferris listed twelve "values for renewal of evangelical theological education," which he adapted from the article by the International Council of Accrediting Agencies for Evangelical Theological Education (ICAA), "A Manifesto on the Renewal of Evangelical Theological Education." Almost all of these values are found expressed in various forms in the accreditation standards of the three main accrediting associations/agencies of Asia.

1. **Cultural Appropriateness** – Training is referenced to the traditions, conditions and needs in the local society, and is responsive to shifts in social norms and values.
2. **Attentiveness** – Basic orientation is toward the constituent church, rather than academia. Input from churchmen is actively sought and is accorded highest priority in development, delivery, and assessment of training programs.
3. **Flexible Strategizing** – Educators are aware of the broad spectrum of training needs which may exist in the constituent church, sensitive to needs which do exist, and creative in responding to needs with appropriate training programs.
4. **Theological Grounding** – The task and guiding values of theological education are derived from, and rooted, in a Biblical theology of creation, redemption, church, and ministry.
5. **Outcomes Assessment** – The value of education is determined by examining alumni performance in ministry (vs. resources and instructional procedures in the training institution).
6. **Spiritual Formation** – A community life is cultivated which promotes and facilitates growth in grace.
7. **Holistic Curricularizing** – Academic, practical, and spiritual training are integrated into a unified program of professional development.

8. **Service Orientation** – Emphasis is placed on leadership as servanthood; elitist attitudes are consciously renounced.
9. **Creativity in Teaching** – Teaching methods are selected reflectively, or developed creatively, to correlate with instructional goals.
10. **A Christian Worldview** – Training seeks to cultivate a mindset in which the Bible is the standard for measuring every area of life and thought.
11. **A Developmental Focus** – Faculty-student interactions are deliberately designed to encourage and facilitate self-directed learning; methods cultivating dependencies are resolutely resisted.
12. **A Cooperative Spirit** – Institutional leadership is committed to open communication and collaboration among evangelical theological education institutions.[26]

The downside of having common standards is a "flattening" of the character of accredited schools so that instead of a *unifying* goal, it could become a *uniform* goal. The curriculum, methodology, etc., of different schools all need to meet the same standards. It is possible that the mission and goal of an individual school may be shaped by these accreditation requirements. It is for this reason that the Asia Pacific Theological Association (APTA) was founded. APTA respects the mission, goals and objectives of different schools and has a commitment to apply the accreditation standards to the "wide range of school and institutional contexts":

> The APTA standards and components provide a useful framework for this effort. The standards are general enough to apply to a wide range of school and institutional contexts. An institutional self-study describes how a school is meeting the

---

[26]Robert W. Ferris, 34-35.

standards in a manner appropriate to its mission, goals and objectives."[27]

Being a latecomer in the theological education enterprise, some among the Pentecostal/Charismatic community did not want the spirituality and mission in their Pentecostal theological education schools to be compromised or shaped by non-Pentecostal accrediting bodies.

Recently, there have been pressures on theological education to seek accreditations from secular agencies, especially government agencies. This has been going on for a while in Western countries where government or regional secular agencies are seen as neutral, and therefore their accreditations are more widely accepted, and thus more valuable. Unless theological education institutions are very clear about their goal of theological education, the mission of the school might be compromised by these accreditations.

The "Stakeholders" of the Goal

Rooy suggests that it is the *laos* (people/congregation of God) who should define the model of theological education.[28] He is therefore implying that the *laos* as the people of God is the main stakeholder in theological education. If we unpack the "prophet-priest-pastor"[29] tri-office anointing paradigm for ministry, and apply that to our unifying goal of producing anointed ministers for the Kingdom of God, we find three different roles of the anointed minister with corresponding stakeholders implied in this teleological model. First, on the "prophet" side, we are talking about a divine call. The second commitment is as a "pastor" to a congregation. Finally, as a "priest," there is a life-long career

---

[27] Asia Pacific Theological Association, "APTA Accreditation Standards," http://apta-schools.org/wp-content/uploads/2013/06/Accreditation-Standards.pdf (accessed on 1st June 2015), 2.
[28] Rooy, 71.
[29] I have changed the office of the King to Pastor to give it a more contemporary relevance. The Old Testament King is considered a shepherd of God's people.

to look forward to. Under these three different roles, there are also three different stakeholders a modern anointed minister should be answerable to: God who calls the prophet, the *laos* (congregation) which the pastor ministers to, and the denomination/tradition which provides the oversight for the minister's career. These are the stakeholders for theological education institutions which have the goal of producing anointed ministers.

A Contextual Model: Mutualities Within Changing Diversities

Conscientization

Kelsey and others have discussed the models of theological education with little reference to local contexts. But, students do not come into theological education as a *tabula rasa* (blank slate). One important difference between secular and theological education is that theological students usually come to study after a life-changing spiritual experience. They do theological education in answer to a divine call. It is my observation that this is especially true of Asian Pentecostal theological education. The training they receive should help them fulfill that call, which means making them relevant and able to minister in a specific context.

In his book, *The 25 Unbelievable Years: 1945-1969*,[30] Ralph Winter talks about the end of Western expansionism in 1945 and how within twenty-five years after that, almost all of the world became sovereign, independent nations. This resulted in the rise of nationalism and the desire to express Christianity in the local people's cultural forms. This was, however, done initially through "uncritical contextualization" resulting in unsatisfying "translated theologies" or, even worse, heretical syncretistic theologies.

---

[30]Ralph Winter, *The 25 Unbelievable Years: 1945-1969* (Pasadena: William Carey Library, 1969), n.p.

Despite the desire for more local and national theologies, theological education continues to be controlled by Western missionaries and patterned after Western models. Many theological institutions simply copied wholesale the requirements and curriculum from the West. Asian theological institutions basically still have the same four-fold curriculum of "Bible, Theology, History and Ministry." Asian theological libraries are still stocked mainly with books from the West. Even in theological institutions that function in the vernacular, many of the books are translations of books written in the West.

The hierarchy of theological awards/degrees in Asian theological education are also patterned and named after Western (American) models. The Asian theologian's academic journey begins with the certificate-level programs and ends up with a variety of terminal degree programs (Ph.D., D.Min., D.Miss, Ed.D., D.Psych., etc.)—not all of which are "theological/religious." The whole journey from a Certificate in Biblical Studies to a Ph.D. can take anywhere between 10 to 15 years, even if one were to study full-time throughout. The theological education enterprise continues to be Western-dominated so that students are willing to pay a premium to study in the West. One common question registrars at Asian theological institutions have to answer is: "Is your institution's degree/credits recognized in America/England/Europe?"

Contextualization & Globalization

There have been constant calls for renewal in theological education in Asia in many conferences and forums, coming as early as the 1938 International Missions Conference where a delegate from India reported:

> Almost all the younger churches are dissatisfied with the present system of training for the ministry and with its results. In many reports received from different parts of the world, it is stated that there are ministers of a poor standard of education,

who are unable to win the respect of the laity and to lead the churches, that some are out of touch with the realities of life and the needs of their people, and are not distinguished by zeal for Christian service in the community.[31]

This repeated call for renewal in theological education resulted in perhaps the most far-reaching reform in theological education and missiology when the Taiwanese theologian, Shoki Coe became the Director of the Theological Education Foundation (TEF). Recognizing the need for change in theological education in Asia, he wrote:

> The search for renewal in theological education had reached the most critical point. We were driven to ask the basic questions: What is theological education? What is it for—not in abstraction but in the setting of the contemporary, revolutionary world, and especially of the Third World which was undergoing drastic changes and crying out for justice and liberation?[32]

Responding to this need, Coe concluded with a call for contextualization in theological education: "So in using the word, contextualization, we try to convey all that is implied in the familiar term indigenization, yet seek to press beyond for a more dynamic concept which is open to change and which is also future oriented."[33] The concept of contextualization is now a powerful impetus for continuing reform not just in theological education but in the mission enterprise as a whole.

But, what about contextualization in a global, pluralistic culture? M. Thomas Thangaraj suggests that globalization and contextualization should be seen in a matrix together. He says, "(W)e are able to recognize

---

[31]International Missionary Council, pp. 188-189, cited by Robert W. Ferris, *Renewal in Theological Education: Strategies for Change* (Wheaton: Billy Graham Center, 1990), 9.
[32]Shoki Coe, "In Search of Renewal in Theological Education" *Theological Education*, 9, 4 (Summer): 233-243, 237.
[33]Coe, 241.

the contextual character of our own theological thinking only when we engage with theologies which have arisen in contexts other than our own."[34] Globalization brings cultures together but also draws out the uniqueness in different cultures.

It is presumptuous to think that simply because of increased travels and contacts with other cultures, we are globalized. Even those who use the language of globalization could themselves be blind-sided by their own parochialism. Writing about the implications of globalization on theological education, Mortimer Arias quoted Mark Kline Taylor and Gary J. Bekker to describe how even those theological educators who use the language of "globalization" are themselves captive to a limiting mindset:

> In short, theological educators who use the vocabulary of "globalization" occupy a social location that (1) is politically privileged both in respect to the world context and within North American society, (2) is economically affluent to the point of having the wealth that gives them access to world travel and comparative analysis, (3) is steeped in an accompanying socio-psychological tension constituted by the contradiction between an awareness of global need and interdependence and an inability by themselves to address the needs of the global context, and (4) is theologically troubled by the demands to rethink the relationship between universality and particularity.[35]

---

[34]M. Thomas Thangaraj, "The Global-Contextual Matrix in the Seminary Classroom," in M. Russsell E. Richey, ed. *Ecumenical & Interreligious Perspectives: Globalization in Theological Education* (Nashville: United Methodist Board of Higher Education, 1992), 110.

[35]Mortimer Arias, "Mutuality in Global Education" in *The Globalization of Theological Education*, eds. Alice Frazer Evans, Robert A. Evans, and David A. Roozen (Maryknoll: Orbis, 1993): 338-350, 344.

Contextualization must therefore go beyond the local classroom walls. Contextualization today needs to be seen in the light of globalization, and a new term has been coined to describe the environment today: *glocalization*. Christians are challenged to come to terms with a glocalized world.[36] Contextualization cannot be done only by the people within the context. Concrete steps must be taken in theological education by all sides of the different global divides: East-West, North-South, etc. Mortimer Arias talks about the need for "mutualities" among the theological education community. These mutualities are what we need to do contextualization in an increasingly globalized world:

(1) Mutuality in Koinonia;

(2) Mutuality in Curriculum;

(3) From Feudalism to Mutuality;

(4) Mutuality in the Faculty Lounge;

(5) Globalization as Mutual Learning;

(6) Mutuality with the Marginalized Minorities;

(7) Mutuality with Submerged Majority;

(8) Mutuality with the Excluded Majority;

(9) Mutuality is Humility in Hermeneutics;

(10) Mutuality in the Classroom;

(11) Mutual Self-Discovery by Immersion;

(12) Mutual Epiphany;

(13) Mutuality in Student Exchange;

(14) Mutuality between Institutions; and

(15) Mutuality in Faculty Exchange.

This list of mutualities is probably not exhaustive. Arias might have included a "mutuality in language/communication" but instead he chose to say towards the end of his article: "To learn another language is a

---

[36]Bob Roberts Jr., *Glocalization: How Followers of Jesus Engage the New Flat World* (Grand Rapids: Zondervan, 2007), *passim*.

concrete form of incarnation and solidarity—a first step in mutuality."[37] This "mutuality in language/communication" should consider the need for theological education in the vernacular languages as well as the digital media. There is a new global internet community of "digital natives" and "digital immigrants" who communicate in their own dialect.

Conclusion

I have chosen to go for breadth rather than depth in this paper. This has allowed me to cast many seed-thoughts (as well as introduce the literature) on the subject of theological education. Many of the thoughts here will need to be further developed at a local level. One of those seed-thoughts that I threw in for this paper is the need to do theological education prophetically (or, "proleptically"); that is, to teach towards and from the future. Being prophetic does not mean being dramatic and sensational. Small but critical and concrete steps can be taken. Incremental changes are often easier to manage. Prophecies in the Bible are not *mere* predictions. Prophetic declarations of the future in the Bible are meant to inspire change in the present to face the future. If I were a prophet, here are some things I would like to "prophesy" for the Asian Pentecostal theological education enterprise (the listing is random and not in any order of importance):

1. There will be increased pressures (from both internal and external sources) to conform to the standards of the world. Not all pressures to change are negative but we must have discernment and always remember that we are called to conform to Christ and to transform the world, and not the other way around.
2. The "evangelicalization" of Pentecostalism will continue. The "secularization" of theological education will continue. This is related to inter-disciplinary or multi-disciplinary approaches

---

[37]Arias, 350.

to education. There will be continuing cross-fertilization and a "flattening of the world."[38] But, when everything is flattened and we no longer have our uniqueness, we will have nothing to contribute in a dialogue. Asian Pentecostalism (as theology and spirituality) must maintain its uniqueness to be relevant.

3. The West will continue its domination of theological education. Unless there are clear and concrete steps taken to affirm the development of Asian faculty IN Asia, we will continue to lose our best potential teachers to the West or have "banana professors"[39] in our seminary.

4. Faculty will continue to come from the West to teach. But, they will come as short-termers and will not have the facilities (funding, language, training, etc.) for life-long commitments to teaching in Asia. Increasing ease of travel and communication will encourage this trend.

5. Asians will continue to have to come to terms with the need to learn English.[40] Korean may be featured in some theological settings but the only Asian language that has the possibility of becoming global is Chinese.

6. Finance will not be an issue. Finance in and of itself has never been, and should never have been, an issue. It is our response to finance that makes it an issue. Many theological institutions sit on very valuable "gold-mine" properties. Institutions must

---

[38]Terminology borrowed from Thomas Friedman, *The World is Flat: A Brief History of the Twenty-First Century* (New York: Farrar, Straaus and Giroux, 2007).

[39]In his book, *Mangoes or Bananas: The Quest for an Authentic Asian Christian Theology*, 2nd ed. (Maryknoll: Orbis, 2014), Hwa Yung used the picture of mangoes (yellow skinned, with yellow flesh) to describe those who are "Asian" both on the outside and inside, while bananas (yellow on the outside but white on the inside) depict those who are ethnically Asian but conditioned by their education to have a Western culture.

[40]There is a language curtain that admits light from West to East, but stubbornly thwarts all theological illumination from East to West. This book is offered, therefore, as an initial attack upon such walls of ignorance now dividing the Church. It is hoped that this study will breach the wall and lead the way to mutually fruitful theological conversation. Carl Michalson, *Japanese Contributions to Christian Theology* (Philadelphia: Westminster Press, 1960), 9.

recognize and tap people who are gifted in finance and administration. This means accepting non-academic colleagues as an integral part of the theological education enterprise.

7. The world will become more visual and digital. The world has gone from concrete to abstract to digital. The digital world, in fact, combines both the abstract and the digital. Students will come as "digital natives" and theological education must respond to that challenge. Our library and delivery methods will be the areas that will be most impacted. Older faculty must become "digital immigrants" to remain relevant.

8. The local church will act like THE Church. Para-churches and sodalities will change. Theological institutions[41] must position themselves as a part of the Church. Some may choose to function within the local church. Those functioning outside the local church structure must find ways to present themselves as a necessary part of the Church and have goals that local churches can identify with.

9. Collaboration will be the way forward. Instead of building and expanding individually, Asian Pentecostal theological institutions will need to come together in symbiotic and synergistic collaborations. This will include the various mutualities suggested by Mortimer Arias.

I am sure there are more "prophetic pronouncements" that can be made but I need to end this paper at some point. We should not be overwhelmed by challenges so that we become *reactive*. Keep the peace that Jesus gave to us: the peace that passes all understanding. It is a peace that the world cannot give. When we have peace, we can take time to

---

[41]See Lee Wanak's discussion on the relationships between theological institutions as sodalities and local churches as modalities, Lee Wanak, "Church and School in Symbiotic Relationship: Toward a Theology of Specialized Institutions," in *Directions in Theological Education* (Manila: OMF, 1994): 69-95.

reflect and then be critically, culturally and creatively *responsive* to changes around us. We must focus on what we have been called to do (goal), go/stay where we have been called to go/stay (context) and God will provide the peace and the resources for us to succeed.

BIBLIOGRAPHY

Print Resources

Amirtham, Samuel and Yeow, Choo Lak. Eds. *Spiritual Formation in Asian Theological Education.* Singapore: ATESEA, 1989.

Banks, Robert. *Reenvisioning Theological Education: Exploring a Missional Alternative to Current Models.* Grand Rapids, MI: Eerdmans, 1999.

Coe, Shoki; Bergquist, James A.; Chou, Ivy; Sapsezian, Aharon: and Tutu Desmond. Eds. *Learning in Context: The Search for Innovative Patterns in Theological Education.* Kent, England: New Life Press, 1973.

Evans, Alice Frazer; Evans, Robert A.; and Roozen, David A. Eds. *The Globalization of Theological Education.* Maryknoll: Orbis Books, 1993.

Farley, Edward. *Theologia: The Fragmentation and Unity of Theological Education.* Philadelphia: Fortress Press, 1983.

Ferris, Robert W. *Renewal in Theological Education: Strategies for Change.* Wheaton, IL: Billy Graham Center, 1990.

Friedman, Thomas. *The World is Flat: A Brief History of the Twenty-First Century.* New York: Farrar, Straus and Giroux, 2007.

Gonzalez, Justo L. *The History of Theological Education.* Nashville: Abingdon, 2015.

Hardy, Steven A. *Excellence in Theological Education: Effective Training for Church Leaders.* Peradeniya, Sri Lanka: Booksurge, 2006.

Hwa, Yung. *Mangoes or Bananas: The Quest for an Authentic Asian Christian Theology.* 2nd ed. Maryknoll: Orbis, 2014.

Kelsey, David H. *Between Athens and Berlin: The Theological Education Debate*. Grand Rapids, MI: Eerdmans, 1993.

Kitagawa, Joseph Mitsuo, Ed. *Religious Studies, Theological Studies and the University-Divinity School*. Foreword by Robert Wood Lynn. Atlanta: Scholars Press, 1992.

Matthaei, Sondra Higgins, and Howell, Nancy R. Eds. *Proleptic Pedagogy: Theological Education Anticipating the Future*. Eugene, OR: Wipf and Stock, 2014.

Menzies, William W. and Carter, John F. *Zeal with Knowledge: The First Forty Years of FEAST/APTS*. Baguio, Philippines: APTS Press, 2004.

Miller Donald E. and Yamamoto, Tetsunao. *Global Pentecostalism: The New Face of Social Engagement*. Berkeley: University of California Press, 2007.

Michalson, Carl. *Japanese Contributions to Christian Theology*. Philadelphia: Westminster Press, 1960.

Nouwen, Henri. *The Way of the Heart: Desert Spirituality and Contemporary Ministry*. New York: Harper Collins, 1991.

Padilla, C. Rene. *New Alternatives in Theological Education*. Grand Rapids, MI: Latin American Theological Fraternity, 1986.

Richey, Russell E. *Ecumenical & Interreligious Perspectives: Globalization in Theological Education*. Nashville: The United Methodist Board of Higher Education and Ministry, 1992.

Roberts Jr., Bob. *Glocalization: How Followers of Jesus Engage the New Flat World*. Grand Rapids: Zondervan, 2007.

Ruokanen, Miikka and Huang, Paulos. Eds. *Christianity and Chinese Culture*. Grand Rapids: Eerdmans, 2010.

Shaw, Perry. Transforming Theological Education: A Practical Handbook for Integrative Learning. Carlisle, UK: Langham, 2014.

Smith, C. Stanley. *The Development of Protestant Theological Education in China*. Shanghai: Kelly and Walsh Limited, 1941.

Smith, Douglas K., Jr. *Training Pastors in the Local Church: Five Models of Theological Education*. Amazon Kindle eBook, 2014.

Stackhouse, Max L. *Apologia: Contextualization, Globalization and Mission in Education* Grand Rapids: Eerdmans, 1988.

Suh, David Kwayn-sun, Meuthrath, Annette, and Choe, Hyondok. Eds. *Charting the Future of Theology and Theological Education in Asian Contexts.* Delhi: Indian Society for Promoting Christian Knowledge, 2004.

Wagoner, Walter D. *The Seminary: Protestant and Catholic.* New York: Sheed and Ward, 1966.

Walker, Louise Jeter. *A Faculty Training Program for Overseas Bible Schools.* Springfield: Foreign Missions Department of the Assemblies of God, 1965.

Wanak, Lee. Ed. *Directions in Theological Education.* Manila: OMF, 1994.

Werner, Dietrich; Esterline, David; Kang, et. al. Eds. *Handbook of Theological Education in World Christianity: Theological Perspectives-Regional Surveys-Ecumenical Trends.* Eugene, Oregon: Wipf & Stock, 2010.

Winter, Ralph. *The 25 Unbelievable Years: 1945-1969.* Pasadena: William Carey Library, 1969.

Yeow, Choo Lak. *ATESEA Occasional Papers No. 7: Challenges and Opportunities in Theological Education in Asia.* Singapore: ATESEA, 1988.

Internet Resources

Asia Pacific Theological Seminary. www.apts.edu.

Asia Theological Association. http://www.ataasia.com/philippines (accessed 4th June 2015).

Association for Theological Education in South East Asia. http://atesea.net/atesea/ (accessed 4th June 2015.

Asia Pacific Theological Association. http://apta-schools.org/ (accessed 4th June 2015).

Browning, Philip. "What is 'Asia'?," Colombia University. http://afe.easia.columbia.edu/ geography/geo_whatis.html (accessed 27th May 2015).

Edgar, Brian. "The Theology of Theological Education." http://brian-edgar.com/wpcontent/uploads/downloads/2010/05/Theology_of_Theological_Education.pdf (accessed 25th May 2015).

Frame-Polythress. "A Primer on Perspectivalism." http://www.frame-poythress.org/a-primer-on-perspectivalism/ for a collection of their works (accessed 25th February 2014).

Hardy, Daniel. https://www.churchofengland.org/media/.../The%20Hind%20report.doc (accessed 25th May 2015).

Hilborn, David. "Beyond Athens and Berlin: Past, Present & Future Models of Theological Education." http://www.stjohns-nottm.ac.uk/assets/Colloquium-Papers/David-Hilborn-Beyond-Athens-Berlin-Colloquium-Paper.pdf (accessed 25th May 2015).

de wit, Willem-Jan. "Theology of Theological Education. http://willemjdewit.com/2013/08/03 theology-of-theological-education-the-athens-berlin-geneva-and-jerusalem-models/ (accessed 1st June, 2015).

The Online Etymology Dictionary. http://www.etymonline.com/ (accessed 1st June 2015).

Illuminating a Canaanite and Judahite Town: The Archaeological Background of Tel Burna

*by Chris McKinny, Benjamin Yang,
Deborah Cassuto, and Itzhaq Shai[1]*

The Tel Burna team would like to offer our heart-felt congratulations to our friend and fellow laborer, Dr. Kay Fountain.

Introduction

Choosing Tel Burna as a Site to Excavate

Tel Burna is an ancient tell[2], located in the Judean Shephelah[3], that was inhabited continuously from the Early Bronze Age, c. (at or about) 3500 BC, until the Persian period, c. 400 BC. In the Old Testament/Hebrew Bible era, the Shephelah was a region peopled by three major polities: the Canaanites, the Philistines and the Judahites.

Tel Burna is located on the northern bank of the Nahal Guvrin, one of five principle east-west oriented valleys in the Shephelah that served as ancient routes connecting the main coastal road, the International Coastal Highway or *Via Maris*, to the Shephelah highlands.[4] In addition, Tel Burna is situated just west of the Azekah-Tel Goded ridge that served as a natural physical border during the Iron Age II between Philistine

---

[1] This study was made possible by support from the Israel Science Foundation Grant No. 522/16 I.S.).
[2] A mound formed from refuse of people living on the same site for thousands of years.
[3] The "Shephelah" is a range of hills between the Coastal Plains and the Jerusalem mountains.
[4] The other four valleys are: the Nahal Aijalon, Nahal Sorek, Nahal Elah, and Nahal Lachish.

Gath and the Judahite towns of the central Shephelah, including Tel Burna.⁵ The tell's important topographical connections, its naturally elevated defensive position (c. 248 m asl (above sea level)) above the surrounding valley (c. 204 m asl),⁶ and its close proximity to the water source of the Nahal Guvrin, demonstrate that Tel Burna was a logical location for an ancient town and therefore promised many rich discoveries.

Since 2009, our team has been exploring the archaeological history of this biblical-era town. So far, the emerging picture from our near decade of investigation is that of a typical late Canaanite and Judahite town of the Shephelah. It appears that its two main periods of occupation were during the Late Bronze Age, from 1550-1200 BC, and the Iron Age II c. 1000-586 BC.⁷ These, as well as the Iron Age I, c. 1200-1000 BC, are the main eras during which the narrative of the Old Testament/Hebrew Bible ostensibly occurred. In addition to its location, this fact was one of the main reasons that we decided to excavate at Tel Burna, since our research interests lay primarily in the Bronze and Iron Ages. Fortunately

---

⁵Contra G. Lehmann and H.M. Niemann, "When Did the Shephelah Become Judahite?", *Tel Aviv* 41, no. 1 (May 22, 2014): 77–94 who argue that the Shephelah did not become Judahite until after the destruction of Hazael; see also discussion in A. Faust, "The Shephelah in the Iron Age: A New Look on the Settlement of Judah," *Palestine Exploration Quarterly* 145, no. 3 (September 2013): 203–219.

⁶This elevated position also made it useful to the Israeli Givati Brigade (as made evident by numerous "foxholes" on the summit) in the War of Independence 1948– see discussion in C. McKinny and A. Dagan, "The Explorations of Tel Burna," *Palestine Exploration Quarterly* 145, no. 4 (December 2013): 300, 304; cf. also A. Dagan and C. McKinny, "The Beginning of Modern Archaeological and Historical Research at Tel Burna," *Moreshet Israel* 12 (2015): 11–29.

⁷J. Uziel and I. Shai, "The Settlement History of Tel Burna: Results of the Surface Survey," *Tel Aviv* 37, no. 2 (2010): 227–245; I. Shai et al., "The Fortifications at Tel Burna: Date, Function and Meaning.," *Israel Exploration Journal* 62, no. 2 (2012): 141–157; I. Shai and J. Uziel, "Addressing Survey Methodology in the Southern Levant: Applying Different Methods for the Survey of Tel Burna, Israel," *Israel Exploration Journal* 64, no. 2 (2014): 172–190; I. Shai et al., "Tel Burna in Iron Age II: A Fortified City on Judah's Western Border," *Judea and Samaria Research Studies* 24 (2015): 27–34.

for us, Tel Burna has very little post-Persian occupation,[8] which allows us to quickly reach our periods of interest in the excavations.

Archaeologists often praise their own sites for their uniqueness; however, another reason that we chose to excavate at Tel Burna was precisely because we did not think that it was unique. Tel Burna was not an ancient capital city, like Jerusalem, or an administrative center, like nearby Lachish. Neither was it a small farmstead or a seasonally inhabited ruin that would have been abandoned at the first sign of trouble (such as an enemy attack, famine, etc.). Instead, Tel Burna, of the Late Bronze Age, and particularly during the Iron Age II, was a typical town situated in an important region between the two dominant regional centers of Gath, located just 8 km to the north, and Lachish located at 7.5 km to the south.[9] Between and around these two centers of power in the Shephelah, were many other sites of varying size and significance also inhabited during these periods: Beth-Shemesh, Timnah, Socoh, Azekah, Mareshah, Tel Goded, Tel Zayit, Tel Erani, Tel ʿEton, to list a few.[10] In the Iron Age II, this geographical situation is highly significant because of the nearby presence of Philistine Gath, the largest city in the entire southern Levant[11] from the Iron Age I until the last third of the 9th

---

[8]Roman and Byzantine remains were found primarily on the eastern and western slopes and in the fields to the south - cf. Uziel and Shai, "The Settlement History of Tel Burna," 230.

[9]It should be noted that the balances of power regularly shifted during these periods with cities like Azekah, Gezer and Ekron, and others dominating the region - cf. e.g., A.M. Maeir and J. Uziel, "A Tale of Two Tells: A Comparative Perspective on Tel Miqne-Ekron and Tell Es-Sâfi/Gath in Light of Recent Archaeological Research," in *"Up to the Gates of Ekron": Essays on the Archaeology and History of the Eastern Mediterranean in Honor of Seymour Gitin*, ed. S.W. Crawford et al. (Jerusalem: Israel Exploration Society, 2007), 29–42; see various papers in A.M. Maeir, I. Shai, and C. McKinny, eds., *"And the Canaanites Were Then in the Land": New Perspectives on the Late Bronze Age of Southern Canaan and Its Surroundings*, in preparation.

[10]For a discussion of these sites, and others, see relevant chapters in C. McKinny, *My People as Your People: A Textual and Archaeological Analysis of the Reign of Jehoshaphat*, American University Studies - Theology and Religion VII (New York: Peter Lang Pub Inc, 2016); C. McKinny, "A Historical Geography of The Administrative Division of Judah: The Town Lists of Judah and Benjamin in Joshua 15:21-62 and 18:21-28" (Ph.D. Dissertation, Bar Ilan University, 2016).

[11]A geographical region encompassing the southern half of the Levant. It corresponds approximately to modern-day Israel, Palestine, and Jordan.

century BC[12] when it was destroyed by Hazael king of Aram-Damascus. This event is described in 2 Kings 12:17.

Tel Burna's location, roughly equidistant between Judahite Lachish and Philistine Gath, meant that it functioned as a Judahite border settlement facing the main international route along the coastal plain from Ashdod in the north, to Ashkelon in the south. This border aspect was another reason for choosing the site of Tel Burna for excavation.

In this paper, we will attempt to illustrate that Tel Burna was one of many typical Canaanite and Judahite towns, and as such, was an integral part of the fabric of the Biblical world. Biblical history, or historiography, as recorded in the historical books of the Old Testament/Hebrew Bible and other ancient sources like the el-Amarna Letters, often focuses on the main centers of power such as Jerusalem and Lachish. However, while not diminishing the significance of these places, the vast majority of ancient Canaanites, Judahites, and Israelites actually lived outside of the principle centers in settlements similar to Tel Burna.

It is important to note that in this article, we will assume a correlation between Tel Burna and the city of Libnah, which appears sporadically in the biblical text, and we will further develop this connection. However, despite this presumed biblical connection, the more enduring significance of archaeological finds from Tel Burna is that they illustrate and illuminate the realities of daily life during the time of the Old Testament/Hebrew Bible.

In what follows, we will first summarize the archaeological remains from Tel Burna, and then discuss the connections between Tel Burna and the biblical world. Our discussion will include a brief overview of the

---

[12]See discussion in McKinny, *My People As Your People*, 115–117; cf. A.M. Maeir, "The Tell Es-Safi/Gath Archaeological Project 1996–2010: Introduction, Overview and Synopsis of Results," in *Tell Es-Safi/Gath I: Report on the 1996-2005 Seasons*, ed. A.M. Maeir, Ägypten und Altes Testament 69 (Wiesbaden: Harrassowitz, 2012), 1–88; A.M. Maeir, "Philistia and the Judean Shephelah After Hazael: The Power Play Between the Philistines, Judeans and Assyrians in the 8th Century BCE in Light of the Excavations at Tell Es-Safi/Gath," in *Disaster and Relief Management - Katastrophen Und Ihre Bewältigung*, ed. A. Berlejung, Forschungen zum Alten Testament 81 (Tubingen: Mohr Siebeck, 2012), 241–262.

identification of Libnah, and an explanation of specific finds that illuminate the daily life of ancient Canaanites and Judahites.

Summary of the Archaeological Remains at Tel Burna

The archaeological remains at Tel Burna extend over a wide area, c. 10 hectares/24 acres, with the main zone of occupation localized at the summit, c. 1.2 hectares/3 acres,[13] and its immediate surroundings to the west, south, and east.

To date, five excavation areas have been opened at Tel Burna with several more areas planned for exposure in future seasons. These include the following: Area A1, a stepped trench with eastern Iron Age II casemate fortifications; Area A2, the center of the summit - Iron Age II and Persian period; Area B2, stepped trench with western Iron Age II casemate fortifications; Area B1, northern end of western lower platform – Late Bronze Age cultic enclosure; and Area C, agricultural installations to the north of the tell.

Area A1 is a stepped trench that is located on the eastern side of the summit. In this area, we exposed a double fortification wall, casemate, that seems to have been built at some point during the Iron Age II, or at least as early as the late Iron Age IIA/9th century BC. It was most likely built at the behest of the Judahite Kingdom. Future excavations will hopefully clarify the dating of the construction of the wall[14] and the political/ethnic affiliation of the city's inhabitants.[15] Following the Iron Age IIB/8th century BC, the inner fortifications in this area were no

---

[13]Including both the inner area of the Iron Age II fortifications and descending slopes that surround them.

[14]Shai et al., "The Fortifications at Tel Burna."

[15]See A.M. Maeir and I. Shai, "Reassessing the Character of the Judahite Kingdom: Archaeological Evidence for Non-Centralized, Kinship-Based Components," in *From Sha'ar Hagolan to Shaaraim Essays in Honor of Prof. Yosef Garfinkel*, ed. S. Galon et al. (Jerusalem: Israel Exploration Society, 2016), 323–340 for a nuanced discussion of the possible relationships between the Judahite monarchy and its subparts (like Tel Burna).

longer used, as several parts of the wall were turned into grain silos during the Iron Age IIC/7th century BC.

Area A2 is located in the center of the summit, and is characterized by a large Iron Age IIB/8th century BC building, at least 15x15 m, that looks to have been the main structure of the town during this period.[16] While it is too soon to be certain of its plan, it is clear that the structure was well built, included at least two monolithic pillars, and had an accompanying large stone-paved courtyard to the north. While this building appears to have been built during the Iron Age IIB, it looks as though it was also re-used during the Iron Age IIC and Persian period up until the late 5th centuries BC. Earlier remains were also found beneath the floor of the structure, which date to the late Iron Age IIA. Since there are clear signs of abandonment at the end of the Iron Age IIB occupation, it would seem logical to connect this event to the campaign of the Neo-Assyrian king, Sennacherib, who attacked King Hezekiah of Judah and his allies in 701 BC (recorded in 2 Kings 18-19). However, we remain cautious about this connection, as we have not yet uncovered clear signs of destruction related to this period, such as have been found at other nearby sites like Lachish.[17]

Area B2 is a stepped trench that is located on the western side of the summit. The excavation of this stepped trench is one of our main long-term goals at Tel Burna. We hope to expose the full stratigraphic sequence of the site in a 10-m wide section from the top of the summit,

---

[16] See discussion in I. Shai et al., "A Private Stamped Seal Handle from Tel Burna, Israel," *Zeitschrift des Deutschen Palästina-Vereins* 130 (2014): 121–137; Shai et al., "Tel Burna in Iron Age II: A Fortified City on Judah's Western Border"; I. Shai, "Tel Burna: A Judahite Fortified Town in the Shephelah," in *The Shephelah During the Iron Age: Recent Archaeological Studies*, ed. Oded Lipschitz and A.M. Maeir (Winona Lake: Eisenbrauns, 2017), 45–60.

[17] This campaign and its aftermath is one of the best attested events in the historical and archaeological record – see e.g., W.R. Gallagher, *Sennacherib's Campaign to Judah: New Studies*, vol. 18 (Leiden: Brill Academic Pub, 1999); A. Faust, "Settlement and Demography in Seventh-Century Judah and the Extent and Intensity of Sennacherib's Campaign," *Palestine Exploration Quarterly* 140, no. 3 (2008): 168–194; Maeir, "Philistia and the Judean Shephelah After Hazael: The Power Play Between the Philistines, Judeans and Assyrians in the 8th Century BCE in Light of the Excavations at Tell Es-Safi/Gath."

near A2, down to the lowest layer of archaeological occupation on the mound at the western lower platform, Area B1.

At the top of the section, we have uncovered what appears to be an Iron Age IIC[18] building, that is a large room within a larger structure measuring 4x9 m and integrated into the pre-existing Iron Age II casemate walls. While this structure appears to be later than the fortification walls, it seems to be indicative of Judahite and Israelite urban town planning. The inner room formed by the casemate walls was incorporated into houses of the "Four-Room" type, which were oriented perpendicular to the fortifications, exemplified by Tel Sheva, Kh. Qeiyafa, etc.

As regards Iron Age II fortifications in B2, we have exposed roughly 2 m of the outer face of the outer wall and have yet to reach the bottom. In this exposure, we found high quantities of Late Bronze Age fill that looks to have been placed there during the Iron Age II to strengthen the fortifications. Further down the slope at c. 5 meters west of the fortifications, we uncovered a fiery destruction layer filled with complete vessels and other important finds. Because we exposed it in one square during the last of week of the 2017 season, it is too early to provide an exact date for this destruction. However, our initial assessment indicates that the destruction appears to be related to the late Iron Age I or early Iron Age IIA, i.e., 11th-10th centuries BC. Future radiometric and ceramic analyses of the remains will help us provide an established date for this impressive destruction layer.

Further to the west in Area B2, it appears that we have the remains of large-scale terracing and perhaps the collapse of a sizable wall, presumably dated to Iron Age II. These can be traced all along the western slope of the tell. Future excavation should clarify the date and purpose of these elements.

---

[18] As in Area A2, the high quantity of Persian pottery and the presence of several intrusive pits indicate the presence of a later Persian occupation in this area.

Area B1 is positioned on the northern half of a platform, c. 40 m wide x 90 m long, located below the summit of Tel Burna. High bedrock, and a very shallow archaeological deposit characterize the plateau. In this area, excavations carried out from 2011-2017 exposed the remains of a large cultic enclosure, Building 29305. This structure is dated to the latter part of the Late Bronze Age, 13th century BC.[19] Building 29305 consists of an enclosure measuring c. 26 m wide from west to east, and at least 24 m from north to south. The outer western side of the structure has a series of rooms near the edge of the plateau, and the inner eastern side has a few scantily preserved rooms near the rise of the tell. The interior of the enclosure can be defined as an open-air courtyard. There were two ovens consisting of a combination of stone pavements, beaten earth surfaces, and bedrock floors. In many locations within the enclosure of Building 29305, the ancient Canaanite inhabitants seem to have used the bedrock as a surface. At one such location, on the western side of this enclosure, we found an impressive assemblage of ritual and prestige-related objects including two ceramic masks, numerous locally-made chalices and goblets, as well as many complete bowls, jugs, and other ceramic forms. Additionally, there were imported Cypriot vessels of various types, including a unique three-cupped votive vessel, with a different type of oil in each cup that was placed intentionally on a flat stone in a deep fissure of the bedrock.[20] There were two enormous *pithoi*[21] of the Cypriot wavy-band type;[22] and a Mittani cylinder seal and scarab bearing the cartouche of Thutmose III, as well as several local and

---

[19] I. Shai, C. McKinny, and J. Uziel, "Late Bronze Age Cultic Activity in Ancient Canaan: A View from Tel Burna," *Bulletin of the American Schools of Oriental Research*, no. 374 (2015): 115–133.

[20] See I. Shai et al., "Trade and Exchange in the Southern Levant in the 13th Century BCE: A View from Tel Burna, a Town in the Shephelah, Israel," in *West and East: Technology and Knowledge Circulation - Idiosyncrasy of Dominant Ideologies in Pre and Early History?*, ed. A.P. da Cruz, in press- for a discussion of these finds in connection with the Late Bronze economic system.

[21] A very large earthenware jar having a wide mouth, used by the ancient Greeks for storing liquids, such as wine, or for holding food, as grain, or for the burial of the dead.

[22] I. Shai et al., "Late Bronze Age Trade as Seen through the Eyes of Two Cypriot Pithoi on a Shephelah Hilltop," *Levant* (in preparation).

imported figurines and zoomorphic vessels.[23] Given the high quantity of cultic and prestige affiliated materials, as well as the large amount of animal bones excavated in this area,[24] it appears that this bedrock courtyard was the focal point of cultic and feasting activities[25] within Building 29305.

Area C consists of several excavated agricultural installations, such as olive and wine presses, that are located just the north of the tell. The close proximity of these installations, as well as the presence of pottery from the Early Bronze Age up to the Persian period, indicates that these installations were used for the production of wine and olive oil throughout the history of occupation at Tel Burna.

Libnah in the Bible

While other site identifications for Tel Burna remain possible,[26] we are relatively confident in the suggestion[27] to equate Tel Burna with the biblical city of Libnah.[28] The evidence for this suggestion is based on several criteria that we have argued for in previous and forthcoming publications that we will briefly summarize here.

---

[23]C. Sharp, C. McKinny, and I. Shai, "Late Bronze Age Figurines from Tel Burna," *Strata: Bulletin of the Anglo-Israel Archaeological Society* 33 (2015): 61–76.

[24]T. Greenfield, C. McKinny, and I. Shai, "'I Can Count All My Bones': A Preliminary Report of the Late Bronze Faunal Remains from Area B1 at Tel Burna, Israel," in *The Wide Lens in Archaeology: Honoring Brian Hesse's Contributions to Anthropological Archaeology*, ed. J. Lev-Tov, A. Gilbert, and P. Hesse (Atlanta: Lockwood Press, Inc., in press).

[25]See discussion in A. Orendi et al., "The Agricultural Landscape of Tel Burna: Ecology and Economy of a Bronze Age/Iron Age Settlement in the Southern Levant" (in press).

[26]See M.J. Suriano, I. Shai, and J. Uziel, "In Search of Libnah," *Journal of Near Eastern Studies* (in press) for alternate suggestions.

[27]The initial suggestion was made by K. Elliger, "Josua in Judäa," *Paliistinajahrbuch* 30 (1934): 58–63; cf. McKinny, "A Historical Geography of The Administrative Division of Judah: The Town Lists of Judah and Benjamin in Joshua 15:21-62 and 18:21-28," 206–209 for the full bibliography.

[28]Uziel and Shai, "The Settlement History of Tel Burna," 242; C. McKinny and A. Tavger, "From Lebonah to Libnah: Historical Geographical Details from the PEF and Other Early Secondary Sources on the Toponymy of Two Homonymous Sites," in *The PEF and the Early Exploration of the Holy Land*, ed. D. Gurevich and A. Kidron, in press; Suriano, Shai, and Uziel, "In Search of Libnah."

1. Tel Burna matches the geographical context of Libnah in the Bible. In the reference to the Israelite military campaign against the southern Canaanite cities, Joshua 10:29-32 indicates that Libnah was near Makkedah (Kh. el-Kôm) and Lachish. Joshua 15:42-44 lists Libnah in the same district as the known sites of Ether (Kh. el-ʿAter), Keilah (Khirbet Qîlā), Nesib (Khirbet Beit Neṣîb), and Mareshah (Tell Ṣandaḥannah). Additionally, Tel Burna's close proximity to Ether, a mere 1.5 km to the north, with which it appears in Joshua 15:55, looks to be evidence in favor of the proposal that Tel Burna equals Libnah. Two other occurrences with geographical details also help undergird the connection between Tel Burna and Libnah. In Joshua 21:13-16,[29] Libnah is listed as one of the Judahite Levitical towns. When it is considered that the Simeonite towns of Ether and Ashan (Joshua 15:42; 19:7; 1 Chronicles 4:32; 6:59)[30] were in close proximity to the Levitical Judahite town of Libnah, one can make the case that this degree of diverse tribal affiliations in a relatively small region is indicative of a border settlement like Tel Burna. This border reality is also highlighted by 2 Kings 8:22 where it records that Libnah revolted during the reign of Jehoram of Judah, c. 853-841 BC.

2. The archaeological finds from Tel Burna match the periods of occupation mentioned in the Bible. As noted above, Libnah is mentioned prominently in the book of Joshua. While the dating and historicity of the narratives in the book of Joshua remain debated,[31] it is particularly striking that the list of "slain kings" in Joshua 12 includes 31 cities. The vast majority of those cities were inhabited during the Late Bronze Age, with only a few notable exceptions that lack Late Bronze Age material,

---

[29]Cf. also the occurrence of Libni and Libnites in Exod 6:16; Num 3:18, 21; 26:59; 1 Chr 6:17, 20, 29.

[30]See McKinny, "A Historical Geography of The Administrative Division of Judah: The Town Lists of Judah and Benjamin in Joshua 15:21-62 and 18:21-28," 109–111, 210–215 for a further discussion of the textual and historical geographical issues.

[31]See e.g., T.B. Dozeman, *Joshua 1-12: A New Translation with Introduction and Commentary* (New York: Yale University Press, 2015), 15–16.

like Arad, Ai, and Makkedah.[32] At the very least, this indicates that Joshua 12, and subsequently Joshua 1-11,[33] represent a "map"[34] that is largely consistent with 13th century BC/Late Bronze Age Canaan. This suggests that these texts are based on an ancient tradition.

More securely, we can clearly date the other biblical references to Libnah to different periods of the Iron Age II. The 9th century BC remains at the site can be related to the revolt of the city during the reign of Jehoram recorded in 2 Kings 8:22; compare (cf.) 2 Chronicles 21:10. The impressive 8th century remains, even without clear signs of a destruction, may be connected to the campaign of Sennacherib in 701 BC. He attacked Libnah after Lachish, and before turning his attention to Jerusalem in 2 Kings 19:8; Isa 37:8. Finally, and perhaps most significantly, are the 7th century BC remains that were found all over the summit, which should be associated with the references to Libnah as the hometown of Queen Hamutal. She was the daughter of Jeremiah, the wife of King Josiah of Judah, and the mother of Kings Jehoahaz and Zedekiah of Judah (2 Kings 23:31; 24:18; Jeremiah 52:1).[35]

3. An earlier form of the Arabic name of Tel Burna might retain a corrupted form of the biblical name Libnah. Tel Burna is the Hebrew name of the ruin that was called Tell Bornâṭ, "mound of the hat," in

---

[32]See C. McKinny, "Examining the Historical Geography and Archaeology of the Slain Kings List of Joshua 12" (in preparation) cf. also the interactive archaeological map of towns mentioned in Joshua 12, https://www.google.com/maps/d/u/0/viewer?mid=1qx8rsHik7dAGdEeujnL8CzDCw6M, (accessed November 6, 2017).

[33]All of the towns mentioned in the narrative of Joshua 1-11 appear in Joshua 12.

[34]Cf. Y. Levin, "Conquered and Unconquered: Reality and Historiography in the Geography of Joshua," in *The Book of Joshua*, ed. E. Noort (Leuven: Peeters, 2012), 361–370, https://www.academia.edu/2404064/Conquered_and_ Unconquered_ Reality_and_Historiography_in_the_Geography_of_Joshua, (accessed November 29, 2014).

[35]Outside of the Bible, Libnah only appears in Eusebius' *Onomasticon* (120.1), where it is said to have been a "village in Eleutheropolitana called Lobana." This Byzantine settlement is most likely located across the valley to the north at Kh. Bornâṭ. For further discussion see McKinny and Dagan, "The Explorations of Tel Burna"; McKinny and Tavger, "From Lebonah to Libnah: Historical Geographical Details from the PEF and Other Early Secondary Sources on the Toponymy of Two Homonymous Sites."

Arabic by mid-late 19th century explorers.[36] However, in 1852 almost two decades before the later explorers, C. Van de Velde recorded the name of the ruin as Tell Bulnab.[37] This form of the name can be understood as a corruption of the biblical name of Libnah by means of metathesis, which is the transposition of sounds or letters in a word.[38]

Objects of Caananite and Judahite Daily Life at Tel Burna

Canaanite Ritual Practice – Feasting, Ceremony, and Symbols

As noted above in our discussion of the remains from Area B1, excavations in this area resulted in the uncovering of Late Bronze Age cultic remains inside a large public building. For readers of the Bible, this is important data for understanding the nature of Canaanite ritual practice. The Old Testament/Hebrew Bible is replete with references to Canaanite and/or Amorite religious affiliations that assign their worship to such deities as Baal, Asherah, and Astarte. Examples of this appear in: Numbers 25:3-5; Judges 2:11-13; 3:7; 6:25-32; 10:6, 10; and 1 Sam 7:4; 12:10. However, in general, these texts do not usually reveal the actual modes and methods of religious expression, neither do they provide much detail regarding the theological worldview of what has been termed a "worldview defined by continuity."[39] To understand the theological framework of the ancient Near Easterner, one must turn to

---

[36] Including Guérin and Conder and Kitchener - see McKinny and Dagan, "The Explorations of Tel Burna," 295–299.

[37] C.W.M. van de Velde, *Memoir to Accompany the Map of the Holy Land* (Gotha: Justus Perthes, 1858), 2.154; C.W.M. van de Velde, "Map of the Holy Land" (Gotha: Justus Perthes, 1865), http://hdl.huntington.org/cdm/ref/collection/p15150coll4/id/7145; see also McKinny and Tavger, "From Lebonah to Libnah: Historical Geographical Details from the PEF and Other Early Secondary Sources on the Toponymy of Two Homonymous Sites" for further support of this occurrence from other 19th century sources.

[38] For an example of this phenomenon see A.F. Rainey and S. Notley, *The Sacred Bridge: Carta's Atlas of the Biblical World* (Jerusalem: Carta, 2006), 183.

[39] See e.g., J.N. Oswalt, *The Bible among the Myths: Unique Revelation or Just Ancient Literature?* (Zondervan, 2009), 47–62.

the Ugaritic Baal Cycle. Although Ugarit is located c. 480 km to the north of Tel Burna, it dates to the same time period and remains the best literary window into Canaanite cult and religion.[40] While the excavations in Area B1 have not added any new theological information regarding the ancient Canaanite cult, we clearly have uncovered an archaeological context in Building 29305 in which Canaanites carried out cultic practices. But what can these finds tell us about Canaanite religion?

First, a fairly large number of people appear to have participated in the ritual activity on the bedrock courtyard in Building 29305, as evidenced by the high quantity of small bowls which were often used for drinking wine, the two large *pithoi* likely used for storing water or grain, and many other vessels such as kraters,[41] Cypriot "milk bowls," and tankards associated with consumption. Taken together with the large assemblage of bones, and the presence of a "relatively high amount of grass pea seeds" on this courtyard,[42] we can conclude that the religious activity involved a common meal consisting of wine, the meat of lamb or goat, and grass peas, as well as other more common grains like wheat and barley.

Second, while we have yet to find an altar within Building 29305, we found at least three static objects in the cultic courtyard that are probably related to cultic symbols. These objects include the following: 1) the Cypriot three-cupped votive vessel in which different oils were placed in each cup; 2) the two massive Cypriot wavy-band *pithoi* sunken into the floor in depressions in the bedrock courtyard; and 3) the three standing stones including the strange rectangular chalk stone with a symmetrical

---

[40]Mark S. Smith, *The Ugaritic Baal Cycle: Volume I* (Leiden: Brill, 1994); Mark S. Smith and Wayne T. Pitard, *The Ugaritic Baal Cycle: Volume II* (Leiden: Brill, 1994).

[41]Krater ancient Greek vessel used for diluting wine with water.

[42]Which appear also at Late Bronze Tel Miqne-Ekron and Tel Batash in contexts that appear to be related to feasting activity. Orendi et al., "The Agricultural Landscape of Tel Burna: Ecology and Economy of a Bronze Age/Iron Age Settlement in the Southern Levant"; A. Mazar, *Timnah (Tel Batash) I: Stratigraphy and Architecture*, Qedem 37 (Jerusalem: Hebrew University, 1997); Yael Mahler-Slasky and Mordechai E. Kislev, "Lathyrus Consumption in Late Bronze and Iron Age Sites in Israel: An Aegean Affinity," *Journal of Archaeological Science* 37, no. 10 (October 1, 2010): 2480–2481.

hole drilled through its center. The massive Cypriot *pithoi* are particularly significant due to their size and origin. Cypriot wavy-band *pithoi* were used as carrying containers in the Late Bronze maritime trade network, and as such, they sometimes appear in coastal sites of the southern Levant.[43] Tel Burna is not a coastal site because it is located more than 30 km from the nearest port, Ashkelon. This signifies that the enormous *pithoi* had to have been carried by an ox-driven cart from a southern Levantine port to Tel Burna, where they were placed inside Building 29305. Therefore, their presence in this building indicates that a large-scale and labor-intensive effort took place to bring them there, pointing to the significance of this cultic enclosure. In fact, there are numerous textual and pictorial examples[44] of ox-driven carts carrying large cultic items. Instances of this practice can be seen in the so-called "Ark Narrative" that is recorded in the Book of Samuel. In 1 Samuel 6, Philistine lords of Ekron returned the Ark of the Covenant to Israel at Beth Shemesh. They placed it on a "new cart" that was pulled by two heifers. In 2 Samuel 6, when David attempted to bring the Ark from Kiriath-Jearim to the city of David, he placed the Ark on a "new cart" that was pulled by oxen. In light of these parallels, and the overall cultic context in this courtyard,[45] we can conclude that the transportation and placement of the two enormous *pithoi* to Tel Burna indicate that these objects became ritually significant when they were placed inside of Building 29305.

Near the *pithoi,* the Cypriot votive vessel was placed in the center of the courtyard on a flat stone, directly beneath the beaded necklace that

---

[43]Cf. e.g., Eric H. Cline and Assaf Yasur-Landau, "Musings from a Distant Shore: The Nature and Destination of the Uluburun Ship and Its Cargo," *Tel Aviv* 34, no. 2 (2007): 125–141; N. Hirschfeld, "The Cypriot Ceramic Cargo of the Uluburun Shipwreck," in *Our Cups Are Full, Studies Presented to Jeremy Rutter*, ed. W. Gauß et al. (Oxford: Archeopress, 2011), 115–120; Shai et al., "Late Bronze Age Trade as Seen through the Eyes of Two Cypriot Pithoi on a Shephelah Hilltop."

[44]See H.A. Layard, *A Second Series of the Monuments of Nineveh: Including Bas-Reliefs from the Palace of Sennacherib and Bronzes from the Ruins of Nimroud* (London: J. Murray, 1853), plate 37 which depicts carts filled with ritual objects driven by oxen.

[45]Shai, McKinny, and Uziel, "Late Bronze Age Cultic Activity in Ancient Canaan: A View from Tel Burna."

included the Thutmose III scarab.⁴⁶ The votive offering's *in situ* location on the floor of the courtyard (that is in a location that could easily be stepped on), as well as the presence of different oils within each cup, would seem to indicate that this was an area of the courtyard that was enclosed in some way, perhaps by a wooden or mud brick barricade. If so, this stone would have served as either a small offering table in which fine oils were offered to a deity, or as a special container in which oils were deposited and then used in a ritual activity. These static symbols appear to be related to specific cultic purposes within these buildings.

Third, there are several smaller objects that appear to have played a role in the cultic activity in Building 29305, namely ceramic masks and fertility figurines. In general, masks have been found across many different periods and cultures.⁴⁷ They are usually associated with cultic activity. The two ceramic masks uncovered in Building 29305 were found together a short distance from both the Cypriot *pithoi* and other cultic objects. The masks were meant to have been worn by humans, probably a priest or priestess, as they fit the human face. They are unlike other examples that are smaller and were meant to either be a small offering or adorn an idol.⁴⁸ While there are no clear examples of masks in the Old Testament/Hebrew Bible,⁴⁹ there is abundant evidence of priests wearing distinctive clothing and accessories that demonstrate their consecration

---

⁴⁶A scarab artifact was an object symbolizing the holy beetle in ancient Egypt.

⁴⁷E.g., H. Pernet, *Ritual Masks: Deceptions and Revelations* (Eugene: Wipf & Stock Publishers, 2006); R. Kletter, "To Cast an Image: Masks from Iron Age Judah and the Biblical Masekah," in *"Up to the Gates of Ekron": Essays on the Archaeology and History of the Eastern Mediterranean in Honor of Seymour Gitin*, ed. S.W. Crawford et al. (Jerusalem: W.F. Albright Institute of Archaeological Research and Israel Exploration Society, 2007), 189–208; E. Stern, "Phoenician Clays Masks from Tel Dor," in *The Fire Signals of Lachish. Studies in the Archaeology and History of Israel in the Late Bronze, Iron Age, and Persian Periods in Honor of David Ussishkin*, ed. I. Finkelstein and N. Na'aman (Winona Lake: Eisenbrauns, 2011), 317–330; E.W. Averett, "Masks and Ritual Performance on the Island of Cyprus," *American Journal of Archaeology* 119, no. 1 (January 1, 2015): 3–45.

⁴⁸Shai, McKinny, and Uziel, "Late Bronze Age Cultic Activity in Ancient Canaan: A View from Tel Burna," 127.

⁴⁹But see discussion in Kletter, "To Cast an Image: Masks from Iron Age Judah and the Biblical Masekah."

and cultic significance, exemplified by the passage in Exodus 28. It is likely that these two masks could have served a similar purpose.

A number of figurines were also found within Building 29305, including several female fertility plaque figurines.[50] Because figurines are typically, although not always, understood to represent deities, one may assume that these figurines were also used for worship at Tel Burna. However, it remains unclear what role figurines played in the actual ritual practices of ancient Canaan. It appears most probable that the female figurines represented a goddess such as Asherah or Astarte, or another female deity. This identification does not necessitate that the figurines themselves were the focal point of religious practice within a cultic setting.[51] Scholars have long recognized that figurines primarily functioned as talismans for personal use, especially for children and women.[52] Thus, the occurrence of numerous figurines and static symbols within the cultic area of Building 29305 provide us a context in which both personal and corporate artifacts of religion were employed alongside each other.

Iron Age Daily Life – Figurines and Weaving

In the middle of Area A2, which is enclosed by the casemate fortification, a large well-built structure was exposed with thick outer walls, encompassing an area of at least 15 x 20 m. The finds within the structure indicate that it should be dated to the 8th century BC. Judahite material culture is noted in the presence of Judean pillar figurines, and typical Judahite pottery, that is parallel to Lachish Level III, the city that was destroyed by Sennacherib in his campaign in 701 BC. The Judahite administrative tools, with their stamped handles, indicate that at least

---

[50] Sharp, McKinny, and Shai, "Strata."

[51] See discussion and criteria in P.R.S. Moorey, *Idols of the People: Miniature Images of Clay in the Ancient Near East (The Schweich Lectures of the British Academy 2001)* (Oxford; New York: British Academy, 2003), 2–3.

[52] See e.g., ibid., 9–11, 21–46; B.A. Nakhai, *Archaeology and the Religions of Canaan and Israel* (Boston: American School of Oriental Research, 2001).

during the 8th-7th centuries BC, Tel Burna was a Judahite fortress (Shai 2017). Due to its size, location, and building technique, one may suggest that that structure that was uncovered in Area A2 was more important than a typical domestic structure, and may have served the local elite at Tel Burna. However, we remain uncertain if this particular building housed the local leadership of Tel Burna, whose allegiance to the Judahite monarchy had been incorporated into the patron-client system of the kingdom.[53]

Within this structure, numerous fragments of Judean pillar figurines (JPFs) were uncovered.[54] In general, these figurines are hand-molded in the shape of a pillar with two knobs representing women's breasts near the top of the pillar. Above this, the head of the figurine was usually depicted with either a pinched face representing the forehead, eye sockets, and nose, or made in a separate mold and attached independently. This latter type usually includes facial features and details such as hairstyles, jewelry, and expressions.[55] Similar to plaque figurines of the Late Bronze Age, both in their purpose and popularity, JPFs appear to be most associated with personal protection as a talisman, and private religion, as opposed to corporate expressions of worship.[56] In short, JPFs are ubiquitous iconic objects that played a cultic, but common, role in the daily life of ancient Judahite women and children in the 8th and 7th centuries BC.

Despite the relative clarity regarding the purpose and contexts of JPFs in scholarship, it is still uncertain if the female form depicted on the JPFs can be related to a specific goddess. Many references in the Biblical text mention Asherah and Astarte. The image of the polemical Ashtoreth

---

[53]Maeir and Shai, "Reassessing the Character of the Judahite Kingdom: Archaeological Evidence for Non-Centralized, Kinship-Based Components."

[54]See e.g., Shai et al., "A Private Stamped Seal Handle from Tel Burna, Israel."

[55]R. Kletter, *The Judean Pillar-Figurines and the Archaeology of Asherah*, BAR International Series 636 (Oxford: British Archaeological Reports, 1996), 1–27.

[56]Kletter, *The Judean Pillar-Figurines and the Archaeology of Asherah*; E.D. Darby, *Interpreting Judean Pillar Figurines: Gender and Empire in Judean Apotropaic Ritual* (Tuebingen: Mohr Siebeck, 2014).

was often described as a tree in the Old Testament passages of Deuteronomy 16:21; Judges 6:25-30; and 1 Kings 15:13. These references, and others, clearly indicate a physical expression of a goddess that was worshiped in a corporate setting within a temple or shrine near an altar. Thus, it seems clear that JPFs cannot be the focal objects of Judahite syncretic religion within these structures. Conversely, it remains possible that JPFs were meant to represent Asherah, Astarte, and other goddesses, such as Hathor, in the sphere of daily life. Accordingly, JPFS can most likely be theologically connected to pagan goddesses mentioned in the Judahite and Israelite prophets' denouncements (as in Micah 5:14), even if they cannot be directly connected to a specific object mentioned in the biblical text.[57]

Iron Age Weaving

The production of textiles is one of the oldest and most complex of ancient crafts. It entails the acquisition and preparation of fibers (typically flax or wool), spinning the fibers into threads, preparing the loom, weaving the fabric, finishing, and laundering or fulling[58] the final product. Dyeing, a complex process in its own right, can be carried out before or after spinning, or on the complete fabric as a whole. Spindle whorls, which are usually made from stone or ceramic material, are the most prominent remains of textile production found in the archaeological record. Spindle whorls are used for spinning, and loom weights are used on the warp-weighted loom for weaving.

Loom weights, found throughout the southern Levant, show that the warp-weighted loom was prevalent in the region from the Iron Age through the early Roman period. At Tel Burna, two groups of loom

---

[57]It is unclear if JPFs can be directly related to the biblical *teraphim* (Gen 31:19, 34–35; Judg 18:17–18, 20; 1 Sam 19:13, 16; 2 Kgs 23:24; Zech 10:2) – see e.g., Karel Van der Toorn, "The Nature of the Biblical Teraphim in the Light of the Cuneiform Evidence," *The Catholic Biblical Quarterly* 52, no. 2 (1990): 203–222.

[58]Process that increases the thickness and compactness of woven or knitted wool.

weights were found in Iron Age II contexts on the summit; one just inside the casemate wall in Area A1, and one in the courtyard of Building 52008 just north of the monolithic pillars.

All of the loom weights were spherical in shape, typical of those found in sites of that period in places like Tell es-Safi/Gath, Tel Azekah, Tel Gezer, Tel Halif, and Tel Batash. Loom weights have been found in both domestic and non-domestic contexts. The evidence for each of these can be seen at Tel Burna. The warp-weighted loom is a vertical loom which was either set up leaning against a wall or set free-standing on an A-shaped frame. Hence, the discovery of a group of c. 40 loom weights found against the inner fortification wall may represent a complete loom *in situ*.[59]

In the biblical passage of Samson and Delilah (recorded in Judges 16:16), Delilah wove Samson's hair into the web of her household loom. The story implies that Delilah's loom was, in fact, the warp-weighted loom. The warp threads of the other looms typical to the region at the time, two-beam horizontal and the two-beam vertical looms, were fastened to fixed beams. The warp of the warp-weighted loom, to which additional warp length can be added by tying extra warp to the weights, is the most likely loom to which Delilah could have incorporated Samson's locks of hair.

The second group of c. 30 loom weights was found in the paved courtyard of Building 52008. They can be understood as representative of a larger-scale textile production. This is based on the loom weights' association with the large (probably administrative) building, and the discovery of a unique plastered installation nearby, and its possible association with textile production. References to centralized, or elite-administered, textile production have been found in Akkadian, Linear B, and Egyptian hieroglyphic texts. In the Old Testament/Hebrew Bible,

---

[59] Further analysis of this group and their context will indicate whether the loom weights were, in fact, compatible to work together on the same loom setup.

centralized weaving on a non-domestic scale is associated with cultic contexts, as in Exodus 35:35 and 2 Kings 23:7.

Conclusion

In this paper, we summarized the Late Bronze Age and Iron Age II archaeological data excavated thus far at Tel Burna. Next, we endeavored to explain the possible direct, and indirect, connections between the archaeology of Tel Burna and the Old Testament/Hebrew Bible. On the direct side, we have shown that Tel Burna is likely related to the ancient Judahite and Levitical town of Libnah that appears in contexts associated with the late Canaanite period in the Late Bronze Age, and the Kingdom of Judah in the Iron Age II. On the indirect side, we demonstrated how the various archaeological finds, and contexts, from Tel Burna can illuminate the world in which the biblical text was written and read. While Tel Burna may not be a uniquely significant site in terms of size or political clout, the material remains that have been uncovered at the site thus far are indicative of the unique Canaanite, Israelite, and Judahite world in which these contexts and objects were created and used.

HOW CAN A MAN READ ESTHER?

by Tim Bulkeley

The biblical book of Esther has provoked widely, and even wildly, differing responses. Esther was not found among the biblical texts from Qumran, nor is it mentioned in the New Testament. It does not appear in the canonical list of Melito of Sardis.[1] Martin Luther wished the book had not survived.[2] Calvin only referenced it once in the *Institutes*.[3] Yet a number of the Church Fathers mention the story with approval, and by the Middle Ages it had already become a Jewish favourite (there are more fragments of Esther from the Cairo Geniza than any other book outside the Torah).[4]

In more recent times (British Prime Minister) Margaret Thatcher was attracted to the book, but commented that it was "gory."[5] Most feminist readers have given this tale, told by men, about a woman, a more negative response. Alice Laffey's evaluation of Esther, especially in

---

[1] Jack P. Lewis, "Esther." In *Encyclopaedia of Early Christianity, Second Edition*, edited by Everett Ferguson, (London: Routledge, 2013), 387 cites Eusebius, HE. 4.26.13fi.
[2] Martin Luther and Alexander Chalmers, *The Table Talk of Martin Luther* (London: H. G. Bohn, 1857), 11.
[3] 4.12.17.
[4] Lewis, "Esther," 387.
[5] Jo Carruthers, *Esther Through the Centuries* (Malden, MA: Blackwell, 2008), 1.

contrast to Vashti, has often been cited and gives a good summary of this sort of reading:

> She is the woman who plays the man's game. Not only does she submit to the beauty contest, she actively participates (2:10, 2:15). Esther carefully follows Hegai's advice on how to accentuate the positive and become the sex object par excellence. Body beautiful (2:2-3, 2:7) and successful sex (2:14) are her tickets to moving up in the world. Esther does not stand with her sister and protest the victimization to which Vashti had been subjected and that might lie in her future as well (2:14); rather, she accepts the rules of the dominant culture and works them to her advantage. She prepares her body for a full year (2:12) to win for it male approval.

This reading of the text suggests that Esther is not the heroine but a victim. She is the stereotypical female who exerts a great deal of effort to produce a beautiful body. She competes against other women for a man.[6]

Supervising Kay Fountain's PhD thesis on Esther was particularly interesting as it allowed me to watch and listen as a woman read this book sympathetically. Usually the Hebrew textual tradition and the ancient Greek version of the Septuagint are the most significant witnesses to the text of Old Testament books. For Esther we have two ancient Greek versions that though similar to each other are also different in interesting ways. Fountain's conclusions recognise, among other things, that the Hebrew text of Esther treats its eponymous heroine differently, for example, highlighting her breaches of customary and conventional gender roles whereas the two Greek texts minimise them.[7]

---

[6]Alice Laffey, "The Influence of Feminism on Christianity," in *Daughters of Abraham: Feminist Thought in Judaism, Christianity, and Islam*, ed. Yvonne Yazbeck Haddad and John L. Esposito (Gainesville, FL: University Press of Florida, 2001), 56.

[7]Allison Kay Fountain, *Literary and Empirical Readings of the Books of Esther* (New York: P. Lang, 2002), 68, 112, 162. Another reason I was delighted to be involved

To talk of Esther as the heroine of the book (as I did in a footnote above), however, is to jump ahead, as the book opens it is by no means clear that this will be so. Esther is not mentioned until 2:7, and then she is presented as dependent on Mordecai. What is even more striking, she does not speak until half way through the fourth chapter, by which stage Memucan (a minor character) has already spoken 78 words, and the king's servants 62. By then also, the villain, Haman, has spoken 33 words. Although Mordecai also does not speak until the middle of chapter 4, he has been mentioned 12 times in chapter 2, 5 times in chapter 3, and 11 times in chapter 4, before he does speak. While Esther has also been mentioned 12 times in chapter 2, she is not named at all in chapter 3 and only 4 times before she speaks in chapter 4. Thus, in terms of both speech and textual focus, in these early chapters the story seems, as Esther's feminist detractors believe, to be about the men.

A traditionally minded (especially male?) reader may therefore be lulled, at the start, into the assumption that this book, like so many others in Scripture, fails to question traditional gender roles. The feminist readers, who have focused on Vashti's rebellion against such a traditional role, may also have been led into such an understanding by these early chapters.

However, the men's extraordinarily exaggerated response to Vashti's refusal of her husband's demand may suggest caution about this conclusion. Memucan's presumption that because the queen has denied the king's authority, all wives begin to "look with contempt on their husbands" (1:16-18), and his even more extreme assumption that once Vashti is put in her place then "all women will give honour to their husbands, high and low alike" (1:20), seem to be accepted with approval by all the men in the text, but seems strangely unrealistic in any real world context. Presumably the customary phallocracy of the Persian Empire had by then been more widely undermined, for by royal decree

---

in that project, the use of empirical investigations alongside "expert" readings, sadly is not reflected in my own essay.

also, "every man shall be master in his own house" (1:22)! If women have been so widely "lacking" in respect to their husbands, will promulgating a law demanding obedience change their attitudes?

Supervising another woman reading Esther added a further dimension to my own reading. Angeline Song approached this book from the perspective of "realistic empathy." Song also engaged with the negative feminist readings of Esther though not primarily by closer reading of the text, but rather by engaging her own story with the biblical narrative. Among other things this perspective of "realistic empathy," her point of view as a colonised woman, sold by her biological parents, learning a mix of Confucian respect and "Asian" humility, lead Song to see how Esther's responses, often perceived as acquiescing to patriarchy, may be her only reasonable manner of resistance, or the "pragmatism of the powerless."[8]

Song's use of the term "empathy" to describe the connection between reader and character, through which the act of reading impacts the reader in deeper than cognitive ways, is in line with the preferences of a number of theorists and psychologists of reading.[9] However, most real readers have preferred talking about their experiences in terms of "identification."[10] Through the process of reading, and the experience of "entering the world" of the characters in a narrative, a text's readers are changed. This is the primary power of the genre of narrative prose. Cognitive Psychologist Keith Oatley sums it up like this: "the process of entering imagined worlds of fiction builds empathy and improves your ability to take another person's point of view. It can even change your

---

[8]See an abbreviated version in Angeline Song, "Heartless Bimbo or Subversive Role Model? A Narrative (Self) Critical Reading of the Character of Esther," *Dialog* 49, no. 1 (March 1, 2010): 56–69.
[9]Susanne Reichl, *Cognitive Principles, Critical Practice: Reading Literature at University* (Gottingen, Germany: Vandenhoeck & Ruprecht, 2009), 109.
[10]Ibid., 110.

personality. The seemingly solitary act of holing up with a book, then, is actually an exercise in human interaction."[11]

Song's approach predicated on "realistic empathy," raised questions for me as a male member of the imperial colonising race, and endowed with the authority of teacher and the title of doctor. With whom could I identify while reading Esther? Readers' identification with characters, and therefore their possibilities of empathy, or even merely sympathy with them, has been widely discussed, but for the most part the criteria remain frustratingly vague. I have been unable to find a discussion of the textual or poetic features in a narrative that might promote empathy or identification with one character or another. However, it seems *a priori* likely that textual prominence would be important (a less prominent character is presumably, all other things being equal, less likely to provoke such a response of empathy).

In their pioneering (and much discussed) *On Gendering Texts* Brenner and van Dijk Hemmes discuss the concept of "voice" in texts. Their interest is in uncovering echoes of the voices of women in texts written by men.[12] However, their list of features that give a character "voice" is interesting as possible indicators of textual prominence. Among other characteristics they note:

> A voice belongs to her/him who holds the primary subject position in a discourse (after that of the narrator but, quite often, as the embodiment of the narrator's privileged albeit covert "voice"). The voice often belongs to and expresses the focalizer of the text. When all or most of the affirmative answers to the questions, Who speaks? Who focalizes the action? Whose viewpoint is dominant? - converge on one and the same textual

---

[11]Keith Oatley, "In the Minds of Others," *Scientific American Mind* 22, no. 5 (November 2011): 62.
[12]Ibid.

figure, then that figure embodies the dominant voice of a passage, be it prose narrative or poetic.[13]

On this basis, I suggest that the characters most spoken about, who speak most, and who are more often the focus of textual interest, are more likely to be empathised (or identified) with. So, turning to the biblical[14] text of Esther, which candidates propose themselves for a male reader to empathise or identify with?

Ahasuerus is the first person to be mentioned. He speaks first, and speaks more words than anyone except Esther. He is introduced first, and presented as ruler of all he surveys and indeed of 127 provinces from India to Cush. Yet, Ahasuerus is a bumbling nonentity, although those 127 provinces must obey his every command (1:1). His counsellors and Esther successively, and easily, bend him to their opinions (1:21 cf. 2:1, 2:4; 3:10; 5:3). Actions that are (presumably) his are often described by the narrator using passive verbs, thus obscuring or diminishing his agency.[15] He may speak more than the other characters; however, as Fountain has noted, almost all of his speech contains questions.[16]

Haman can be resisted as object of empathy, for despite being a melodramatic villain, he is also an evident fool. As villain, he is a desirable character for Jewish children to play, in Purim re-enactments of the story, but such a caricature of the blind idiocy of evil is hardly an appropriate role model for a reader's life.

Mordecai is a more promising candidate. He is a Jew, and thus ideologically and ethnically aligned with the narrator. He appears in the

---

[13] Athalyā Brenner and Fokkelien van Dijk Hemmes. *On Gendering Texts: Female and Male Voices in the Hebrew Bible* (Leiden: Brill, 1996), 7.

[14] At this point I am only considering the Hebrew text on which most English translations are based considering this to be the "biblical" text of Esther (while realising that many Christians across time and space, notably members of Eastern Orthodox churches, will disagree), I will add some comments on the Greek versions of the story below.

[15] Fountain, *Literary and Empirical Readings of the Books of Esther*, 160.

[16] Ibid., 136.

narration before Esther (Mordecai is introduced at 2:5 and Esther herself only at 2:7, as his dependent orphan cousin and ward). He is named 58 times (far more than the king, who is named only 30 times), indeed more than Esther, his ward (55 times), and at the end of the book he is elevated to second position in the empire, after king Ahasuerus (10:3), while Esther is not mentioned at all in the final chapter of the book that bears her name. At the start of the story, as we might expect of a dutiful ward, Esther follows Mordecai's advice (2:10), and he protects her (2:11). However, as the tension mounts his role becomes less significant. At the start, he uncovers a conspiracy and uses Esther as a channel to communicate this information to the king (2:21-23). In chapter three he bravely refuses to offer quasi-divine homage to Haman. But in chapter four, when the genocidal decree is promulgated, he is reduced to merely mourning in sackcloth. Only when Esther sends the king's eunuch Hathach to prod him is he moved to constructive action, and at the close of the chapter the roles of the two Jewish characters are reversed, and he goes and does "everything as Esther had ordered him" (4:17). It is true that in chapter six he is again extravagantly honoured, but this pantomime serves more to humiliate the villain, Haman, than to present Mordecai himself as a role-model, and following Haman's hanging, Mordecai is honoured because of his family relation to Queen Esther, again a reversal of roles as she has become his protector and sponsor.

Recognising this relative dearth of male role models reminded me of my experience as a teenager on first reading Jane Austen's classic novel *Pride and Prejudice*. Like most readers I found myself experiencing events through the eyes of Elizabeth Bennet. Although she is not the narrator of the story, the narration usually follows her. The reader, in identifying with her, comes to share, and perhaps to understand, Elizabeth's frustration and sense of being stifled by the social roles expected of unmarried young women at that time and place. Seeing sympathetically (that is by experiencing them "with" her) the constraints on Elizabeth, a male reader is invited to consider how his own society's social expectations restrict and limit women.

Indeed, if Fountain and Song have correctly identified the features of the book of Esther, then the eponymous heroine both sometimes transgresses expected gender roles, and sometimes complies with the expectations placed upon her on order to achieve her goal (saving the Jewish nation from intended genocide). In this she always operates within a cultural setting that severely limited the behaviour expected of a "proper" woman. A reader who approaches the book identifying with Esther can hardly escape some sense of the confining and restrictive effects of these cultural expectations.

However, such a reading of Esther depends on an understanding that the Hebrew text itself offers such resistance to socially expected roles. As I noted in passing above, some feminist scholars believe that this book functions rather in support of such expectations. To my mind, one of the strongest evidences against their claims was presented in Fountain's thesis. The two Greek texts mentioned earlier,[17] when compared with the Masoretic Text, offer consistently greater conventional religiosity (most notably by mentioning God, but also through characters praying to God), and they also present Esther as acting more in accordance with conventionally expected feminine roles (for example by showing less initiative). Even the differences in the order of presentation of information serve to highlight males in the Greek texts by comparison with the Hebrew.[18]

If we add to this the evidence of religious resistance to the inclusion of this book in the canons of Scripture, we can conclude that since early times the book has been perceived as too little religious. It is therefore no

---

[17] For more information see e.g. Kristin De Troyer, "Esther in Text- and Literary-Critical Paradise," in *The Book of Esther in Modern Research*, ed. Leonard Greenspoon and Sidnie White Crawford (London: A&C Black, 2003), 31. Both Greek texts present a number of additional sections, and well as other smaller adaptations of the traditional Hebrew text.

[18] Fountain, *Literary and Empirical Readings of the Books of Esther*, e.g. 31-34.

surprise that the Greek texts, if they are seen as secondary adaptations, as most scholars do see them, should take steps to "rectify" this omission. That these texts also take steps to rectify the narrative in the direction of having Esther behave in more conventionally acceptable ways, and by giving the men more prominent and dominant roles, therefore strongly suggests that the Hebrew Text was perceived, consciously or unconsciously, to go too far in presenting Esther as the focus character, and too much initiative.

Such a tendency to adapt the telling to conform the book to conventional gender roles is also evident in modern retellings aimed at children. *Veggie Tales* are a series of animated videos retelling Bible stories for children. Although owned by DreamWorks Animation (a secular company) the fact that the videos are marketed at Christian parents (particularly Evangelicals and Pentecostals) suggests that as well as entertainment value (note the references to pop culture for example) "faithfulness" to the Biblical text is likely to have been a consideration in the production, so any deviations from that text are of interest.[19]

The 14th *Veggie Tales* episode, "Esther... The Girl Who Became Queen," adapts the story of the book of Esther.[20] The adaptations in the Greek versions make the religious elements more explicit. The adaptations in *Veggie Tales* do this even more strongly. These changes may not at first seem to function as a means of increasing Mordecai's role at the expense of Esther's, as the Greek changes did. However looking more closely at the changes suggests a cumulative effect. The Hebrew text may suggest that Mordecai had a hand in instructing Esther, as his ward, about life and morals, but there his role as mentor is not made explicit. By contrast from the start of the video version we watch as Mordecai

---

[19] I assume the scriptwriters were working from memory of or access to common English Bibles, which render the Hebrew text, and not to either Greek text.
[20] Already the title suggests the direction of the adaptations, for Esther becomes queen in the middle of the second chapter, while much of the remainder of the book presents her as saviour of her people. *Esther: the Girl Who Became the Saviour of Her People* might be thought a less gender biased title!

instructs Esther, thus his authority as guardian is highlighted, preparing for the later changes.

The biblical book (in the Hebrew text on which most English translations are based) highlights issues of gender relationships near the start of the book. Vashti's refusal to obey her husband and the men's fear of such "rebellion" (1:18) is the heart of the opening chapter. Indeed the extravagant response of the men to her disobedience is often noted and commented upon. In the *Veggie Tales* video version, the reason that Ahasuerus needs a new queen is left obscure, thus the issue of women refusing to obey men is removed from prominence in the story.

When Esther is in the palace, the telling in the Hebrew highlights her common sense and her initiative. These things show her wisdom as well as gaining her favour.[21] In the video, her rise to favour seems to be attributed solely to her ability to sing well.[22] During her early days in the royal harem, Mordecai's role as her mentor and advisor is much increased in the *Veggie Tales* version, by comparison with the biblical telling. Here the "boys" side with each other, as Mordecai tells her that Ahasuerus is "sharp, real sharp." They do this although, as in the Bible, in this telling he manifestly is not at all "sharp!" In the video, Esther speaks no more than Haman and Mordecai do.[23] In this version, the male villain Haman is given a solo like the heroine Esther. The Hebrew Bible telling of the story where Esther speaks more than any male character stands in stark contrast to this. There the most loquacious male is Ahasuerus with 148 words, Haman the villain speaks 121, and Mordecai a mere 25 words, while Esther speaks 182 words!

In *Veggie Tales,* once Haman's plot is revealed, Mordecai takes the initiative by informing Esther of what is going on, by contrast in the Bible at the start of chapter four he sits in mourning, and tells Esther nothing.

---

[21] Song, "Heartless Bimbo or Subversive Role Model? A Narrative (Self) Critical Reading of the Character of Esther," 60-1.

[22] Perhaps a de-sexualised version of the Esther of many feminist readers, who rises merely because of her appearance.

[23] I did not attempt to count the words, but the effect seems obvious.

There she must take the initiative by sending messengers to inquire about the meaning of his behaviour when it is reported to her. Mordecai again speaks more than Esther in the video version, and offers to call for prayer on her behalf. In the Bible version, it is Esther who uses her own authority to command prayer and fasting from the Jewish community. This religious intercession is not mentioned as being for her own needs, indeed it is implied that the people request divine aid for the community. In many ways the video retelling of this scene makes Esther an obedient ward to Mordecai, as traditional roles might suggest, instead of the reverse, as the Bible recounts, and also presents her as concerned primarily for her own needs.

In sometimes small, but in often obvious ways, this modern adaptation of the story of Esther presents its central character as more submissive than the Bible does. It also seems to avoid picturing the occasions where she takes the initiative, or frankly ascribes such initiating to a more suitable, namely a male, character—usually Mordecai. These changes are not as strong and clear as the adaptations that were made because the telling is aimed at young children. Examples of these include replacing execution by banishment to the "Isle of Perpetual Tickling," and removing all sexual tension from the story. Yet despite not being the biggest adaptations, by removing Esther's initiative and by minimising her breaches of conventional roles, a pronounced cumulative effect results in domesticating this biblical heroine. The book is made safe for male readers expected to live out conventionally gendered roles.

The book of Esther has often been the subject of controversy. Rabbis who mistrusted its failure to speak of God questioned its holiness. Luther by contrast distrusted its partisan Jewish character. Once one recognises the ways in which this book gently highlights Esther's initiative and her authority, especially since this follows after Vashti's more overt challenge to male dominance, one may discover another reason to suspect this "dubious" biblical book. Most retellings of the book, by both ancient and modern storytellers, tend to reduce the power of elements of the book's message that seem "difficult" to make it more palatable.

Some diminish Esther to a conventional girl called by her beauty and grace to assist Mordecai in saving the Jewish nation. They may make the book easier for male readers, but they diminish its power as they diminish its challenge. As well as providing a good tale for Purim pantomimes, this book also questions the assumptions made by patriarchal cultures about the respective roles of women and men.

A true though masculine reading of Esther then, will empathise with the young queen's struggles, wisdom, and courage. It will recognise how she operates within constraints set by convention even as she stretches the boundaries those constraints impose. It will be aware that her need to be effective forces her to comply with some demands of convention. Above all, such a reading will need be more supple in its own gender stereotypes and expectations than either *Veggie Tales* or the Greek translators were. Indeed, it will need to allow these stereotypes to be bent. In this process we male readers of Esther can learn to see the world as others see it, and recognising the limits on her actions we will see queen Esther, as the girl who became the saviour of her people.

NAVIGATING THE EMPIRE: ESTHER AS A MODEL OF MARGINALISATION

by Dr. Jacqueline Grey

There is no doubt that, to women and men in the Asia and Pacific region, Kay Fountain has been a model of a pioneer academic and practitioner. Fountain began her academic career when few Pentecostals were in quest of higher education. She has blazed a trail for Pentecostals to engage in intellectual pursuits while maintaining their vibrant spirituality. Yet, while Fountain has championed education, she has also demonstrated practical application. Alongside her academic career, she has been an active minister and practitioner, demonstrating that she "walks the talk" of what she models to her students. The impact of Fountain's work cannot be underestimated as she has provided inspiration and example to so many.

I personally have been inspired and encouraged by the career and ministry of Kay Fountain. As a female academic, she has been a model to me of a godly and self-sacrificial woman who ministers with excellence. In particular, she has encouraged many through her research on the Book of Esther. So it is in her honour that I would like to explore the topic of modelling and mentoring in the Book of Esther. While it may be questioned if Esther was a role model for marginalised Jews during the Diaspora, there is no doubt that Fountain has been a model to women and men of a spirit-filled academic and practitioner.

Introducing Esther

The geographic displacement of segments of the Judean community as part of the Babylonian invasion is a disturbing yet pivotal episode in the Old Testament writings. The experience of the Judeans is captured in various expressions from narrative to poetry, including lament, historical testimony, autobiography, prophetic oracle, and prayers. These diverse writings each contribute to create a picture of exile and to frame what it might have looked like as part of the Judean experience. "Exile," is a loaded term. It can refer to geographic displacement, psychological dislocation, religious separation, and/or political or social isolation. However, I would suggest that it is the character portrayal of Esther that captures most vividly the reality of exile with all of its diverse meaning. Esther is introduced in the narrative as an example of ultimate marginalisation. She is an orphan girl exiled from her homeland and into the harem of a Gentile king—thereby doubly exiled.[1] Yet despite her disadvantage, she utilises all her resources to reverse her situation. The narrative describes the movement of Esther from social marginalisation to being at the centre of the Empire.

This paper will explore how the character of Esther is a model for Jews living in the Diaspora as they attempted to navigate the Persian Empire. She is confronted with the challenge of either adopting or rejecting the Empire's culture. Unlike other characters such as Daniel, she demonstrates a willingness to compromise (or adapt) to avoid persecution. This figure of Esther will be contrasted with the marginalisation of the Pentecostal community. Like Esther, the origins of Pentecostalism are a narrative of marginalisation. The minority communities, particularly the Assemblies of God in Australia and the United States, developed outside the boundaries of the broader and "respectable" religious and secular communities. Marginalisation or

---

[1] Carol Betchel, *Esther*, Interpretation, (Louisville, Kentucky: John Knox Press, 2002), 30.

social exile was part of their identity as the faithful sought to separate from "the world" and from those opposed to the Gospel. However, like that noted in the narrative of Esther, there has been a shift in the narrative of Pentecostalism. In recent decades, it has been moving away from its psychological and cultural marginalisation and proactively seeking to be at the centre of the social and political community. In the light of this shift, what can the narrative of Esther offer the current Pentecostal community as it seeks to navigate the Empire?

Setting the Narrative

The narrative of Esther is set in the Diaspora, with all of its exotic descriptions of harem life and Persian bureaucracy. It presents a reflection on life for exiled Jews. Some of the peculiarities of life in this context include particular Jewish practices, such as fasting, as well as the conspicuous absence of God and the land of Israel in the narrative of the Masoretic text. While debate continues as to whether the Book of Esther was actually written in the location and period of the Diaspora (Stern, for example, presents a compelling argument for the Judean provenance of the Hebrew text), the actual setting of the narrative is clearly the Persian court.[2] The narrative is part of the broader testimony of the people of Israel—a testimony that began in Babylon[3] when Abraham was called to leave his homeland to become an exclusive worshipper of Yahweh. However, by the time of Esther, the journey had led the Israelites from living in the land of promise to being exiled back to Babylon.

The narrative of Esther is located in Susa, one of the capitals of the Empire. Yet while many characters of the Old Testament chose to return to the land of promise and help re-establish the Judean community,

---

[2]Elsie Stern, "Esther and the Politics of Diaspora." *Jewish Quarterly Review* 100, No. 1, (Winter 2010), 23-53.
[3]Specifically, Genesis 11:21 refers to Abram being originally located in "Ur of the Chaledeans." This is generally identified as being located in the southern portion of Babylon or Mesopotamia. However, to emphasise the geographic connections in the narrative, he is referred to as being from more generally the region of Babylon.

Mordecai and Esther chose not to return but to stay in the Persian capital. They remain in exile not only geographically, but also socially. Mordecai is of the house of Kish—a veiled reference to the strongly shamed and discredited house of Saul. One of the most disreputable acts of Saul was sparing Agag, king of the Amalekites (1 Sam 15) in disobedience to the prophetic word. This reference is important in order to understand the enmity between Mordecai the Jew and Haman the Agagite because it reflects the ancient rivalry. According to Berger, the selection and function of Esther is to restore the reputation and honour of the line of Kish.[4]

Hidden Identities

The character of Esther is first introduced as the orphan cousin of Mordecai, who had been carried into exile from Jerusalem by Nebuchadnezzar. It seems that Esther (or Hadassah) has lost her parents and her name. Hadassah means 'myrtle'—a tree of restoration used in Isaiah 55 to picture the transformation of the desert from thorns to flourishing. Esther most probably means "star," pointing to the Babylonian goddess Ishtar. As Betchel notes, it is almost as if a double identity is set up from the beginning, she being both grand Gentile goddess and humble Hebrew flower.[5] This dualistic identity perhaps emphasises the Diaspora dream—to embody both the Gentile power and Jewish holiness. Throughout the narrative, the exiled girl is known as Esther. In fact, she not only is exiled from the land but also taken into the harem of the King. She is vulnerable to the circumstances around her.

Esther is the very picture of powerlessness—an orphaned female Jew living in Persia who is taken into the King's possession. She accepts life in the harem, which the previous "star" Queen Vashti, had rejected with spirit. Yet it is this very lack of power that makes her a paradigm of the

---

[4] Yitzhak Berger, "Esther and Benjamite Royalty: A Study in Inner-Biblical Allusion." *Journal of Biblical Literature* 129 (2010), 625-44.
[5] Betchel, 30.

diaspora Jew. While Mordecai is identified as a Jew, for some reason knowledge of this ethnicity is dangerous, so Esther is advised by her guardian to keep this information quiet. She then exists in the harem as any other hostage. Nothing distinguishes her Jewishness except this secret known only to a few.

The Jewishness of Esther does not seem to have an effect upon her actions, behaviour, or worldview. Unlike Daniel, she does not follow the food laws, pray (in the Masoretic Text), or express interest in Jerusalem. She accepts her position in the king's harem and docilely submits to sexual relations with a Gentile to whom she is not married. She is not distinguished from the other women in the harem, other than a sense of graciousness that endears her to others (2:15). Esther functions as a model citizen, demonstrating complete obedience to Persian law and customs. This is important in the narrative because later, Haman accuses the Jews of not keeping the King's laws (3:8). Similarly, Mordecai, a royal courtier, progressively rises through the ranks of Persian court life despite his known identity as "Mordecai the Jew." Being a Jew does not appear to be an obstacle to a successful life and position of influence. In fact, when Haman's edict is announced in Susa, the city is described as being bewildered (3:15)—not hostile, simply confused.

However, is this lack of Jewishness presented in the Esther narrative a positive portrayal of Diaspora living or, as Stern suggests, a comic farce to ridicule this false utopian dream of dualistic living? Does Esther compromise too much? The context that prompts the revealing of Esther's ethnicity is the threat of extermination. Once faced with annihilation, she must chose either to identify with "her people" (8:6) or to reject her ethnicity. Calculated by the enemy of the Jews, Haman, the threat of annihilation develops as the key conflict in the story. As noted above, his hatred is not solely founded on the contemporary behaviour of a single Jew (Mordecai) but is based on an ancient tribal enmity. While Esther may think she can hide in the palace, as Mordecai boldly warns her, she will be found out eventually.

When Mordecai challenges Esther that perhaps she has "come to royal position for such a time as this," he presents her appointment as Queen positively. He challenges her that she, a Jew, will not be exempt from this extermination, even in the palace. Mordecai requests her help in this message passed on by her servants: "Do not think that because you are in the king's house you alone of all the Jews will escape. For if you remain silent at this time, relief and deliverance for the Jews will arise from another place, but you and your family will perish. And who knows but that you have come to royal position for such a time as this?" (4:13-14). As Saul shamefully lost his opportunity to reign, so Esther may lose the opportunity to redeem her family name. Perhaps another from the house of David might rise to take her place.[6] To claim her opportunity, she must act boldly and decisively.

One of the great ironies in this section is that Haman's proposal to the king stated that the Jewish people were law-breakers, yet Esther is reluctant to help because it will mean breaking the law. However, to save her and her people from an edict based on them being alleged law-breakers, she must violate it. She rises to the challenge by ordering a three-day fast, after which she will go to the king unsummoned. By this action, she will potentially suffer the same fate as her predecessor, Vashti. Yet she determines to go to the king, even though it is against the law—"and if I perish, I perish" (4:15-16). By her actions, Esther associates with the Jewish people. In deciding to appeal to the king, she makes her and her people as one.

Like the Book of Esther, the Book of Daniel also contains a narrative of court conflict. They both navigate successfully the traps of their enemies to become powerful and feared figures by the resolution of the narrative. The key problem by which both Esther and Daniel are exposed is their "Jewishness." While Esther remains initially hidden, it is only time, as Mordecai threatens, before her secret is revealed. It is this exposure that proves critical to her actions. The enemies within both

---

[6]Berger, 635.

narratives display a hostility to the national identity of the heroes. However, unlike Esther, it is Daniel's piety that his enemies use to propel the conflict, which is subsequently resolved by God's active intervention.[7] Yet, through their clever navigation of the conflict, the situation is reversed so that both Esther and Daniel emerge with position and influence that is desired by Jew and non-Jew alike. They emerge to find their place in a Gentile world. This place is both part of the Gentile culture and yet not incompatible or untrue to their own national and cultural identity. Even when Esther reveals her Jewish identity to the King, he does not balk at promoting her political power.[8] Instead, he continues to gift her political demands (8:3-4; 9:12-13).

Yet despite the persecution, both Daniel and Esther do not present a critical perspective of the foreign court. They continue to exhibit a level of fidelity to their Gentile kings. The loyalty of Esther and Daniel is dualistic—i.e., they support both the Jewish people and the Persian king. This paints a portrait that Diaspora life outside the land of Israel was both successful and meaningful.[9] It is successful in that they rise to positions of influence; it is meaningful in that they, particularly Esther, use their influence for the benefit of the Jews living in the land. As Kay Fountain notes, "When a person comes into a leadership position, it is not merely for their own benefit, but for the fulfilment of God's purposes and the protection of God's people."[10]

---

[7] W. Lee Humphries, "A Life-Style for Diaspora: A Study of the. Tales of Esther and Daniel." *Journal of Biblical Literature* 92 (1973), 219-220.

[8] Stern, 42.

[9] Ibid., 29. According to Stern, the message of Esther is not a defense of Diaspora living, but "a comic critique of it" (p. 31). Yet, this anti-reading still places the narrative in the setting of Diaspora.

[10] A. Kay Fountain, "Canonical Messages in the Book of Esther," *Journal of Biblical and Pneumatological Research*, Vol. 2 (2010), 3-17.

Esther's Transformation

The exchange between Esther and Mordecai in Chapter 4 marks a shift both in the story and in the character of Esther. The narrative at this point is now told from the perspective of Esther. She is sending clothes to him and sending messengers to him and having messages reported back. She is authoritatively making commands. In calling for the fast, she assumes the role of a national and religious leader. Through this exchange with Mordecai, we see Esther emerge as a leader and hero for the Diaspora community. Mordecai begins to treat her not as his adopted daughter who should be obeying him, but as a partner and equal. Rather than being passive, she acts as an initiator and planner. That once-passive, marginalised girl becomes transformed into an active and powerful woman who saves her people. Now a model of courage and self-sacrifice, she ruthlessly sacrifices her enemies.

The conclusion of the Book of Esther presents a complete reversal—i.e., those without power (Esther) emerge powerful. She emerges as the awesome Gentile goddess who annihilates her enemies in turn and completes the destruction that Saul refused. By the end of the story, we see her take her full role as "Esther the Queen." She stands as a peer with Mordecai as they direct the wealth of Haman and execute unrelenting vengeance. Yet she maintains, in fact re-discovers or re-invents, her Jewish past, in Chapter 9 being referred to as "Queen Esther, daughter of Abihail . . . " At the conclusion of the story, after she has both acted and spoken for herself, we discover that her father's name is Abihail, "my father is Strong"[11] She retrieves her heritage, adding legitimacy to her royal lineage through the redeemed name of the house of Saul, and reverses her previous familial exile and orphan state. She is now daughter and queen, no longer marginal but standing at the centre of the community. Through the seeming coincidences of the narrative

---

[11] My thanks to Dr. Lee Roy Martin for this insight.

coincidences that many scholars emphasise as the providence of God, Esther is now a key influencer in the land. She is the Jewish Diaspora dream incarnate.

Pentecostals and Esther

Like Esther, the Pentecostal community has been in social exile. When Pentecostalism first emerged within, among others, the North American and Australian landscape in the early 19th century, it was marked by marginalisation and rejection from the "respectable" society, including most other established denominations. A movement led mainly by the poor, socially marginal, academically uneducated, and some women,[12] it was not acceptable to the conservative Western society, both religious and general.[13] It was exiled as "strange," "emotional," and lacking the correct objectivity expected by the religious community. This marginalisation was considered by the fledgling movement as a reflection of the depravity of the "world" and seen by the movement as a sign of the imminent return of Christ.

According to Grant Wacker, Pentecostals were certain they were riding the crest of the wave of history that would involve them directly in the intervention of God and be marked by an intensification of the divine presence and experience of the Holy Spirit for healing, global

---

[12]By 1925, 11of the 18 Pentecostal churches planted in Australia were founded by women. Even by 1930, 20 of the 37 churches (for which information is available) were initiated by women. Barry Chant, 'The Spirit of Pentecost: Origins and Development of the Pentecostal Movement in Australia, 1870-1939.' Thesis for Ph D, Macquarie University, 1999, 428.

[13]Unlike the Assemblies of God in America, which began among the urban and the working classes, the movement in Australia originated among middle-class and rural groups, who were not academically educated. According to Chant, ". . . in Australia, its origins were among people of relatively comfortable socio-economic status" (p.38). Chant demonstrates the middle-class beginnings of Pentecostalism by a comparative study of occupations, which ". . . shows that the percentage of Pentecostals involved in professional occupations in the 1930s was roughly double that of the community while the percentage of labourers was approximately half."[13] See Chant, 38.

evangelism, and spiritual warfare.[14] In this apocalyptic-type worldview, the faithful must endure "this present evil age" in expectation of future glory. Their worldview and sense of persecution was reflected in the eschatological and apocalyptic emphasis of their writings and limited literature. As Hanson notes, the experience of alienation or times of crisis is the sociological context from which many feel gives rise to apocalypticism.[15] This worldview is not unlike that observed in the visions of Daniel. Like the Diaspora community, they were marginalised and expected to navigate that marginalisation.

These origins have profoundly affected the worldview and theology of contemporary Pentecostalism globally. Because of its orientation toward the supernatural, Pentecostalism has flourished predominantly in the non-Western context, such as South America and parts of Africa. However, as Pentecostalism has increased numerically over the last few decades,[16] so also has its aspiration for increased social stature and political influence. This is observed particularly in the Australian context. The process of institutionalisation and adoption of wider cultural norms by a previously marginalised group in order to achieve social respectability has been the focus of various studies in Pentecostalism globally—a process from which the Pentecostal movement in Australia has not been immune.[17]

---

[14] Grant Wacker, *Heaven Below: Early Pentecostals and American Culture* (London: Harvard University Press, 2001), 251-65.

[15] Paul Hanson, *Old Testament Apocalyptic* (Nashville: Abingdon Press, 1987), 75.

[16] According to Assemblies of God statistics (the largest Pentecostal movement in Australia), they currently consist of more than 1,000 churches with over 160,000 constituents.

[17] In particular, the study of Margaret Poloma on the A/G in the USA represents this attempt to capture the sociological changes within the global movement. M. Poloma, *Assemblies of God at the Crossroads: Charisma and Institutional Dilemmas* (Knoxville, TN: University of Tennessee Press, 1989).

From the Margins to the Centre

The substantial numerical growth and subsequent process of institutionalisation in the Australian Pentecostal movement has been a double-edged sword. While it has meant the introduction of stabilising factors, such as training institutions and the formulation of doctrine, there has also been a loss of the earlier revival spirit linked to the immediacy of the *parousia*. As Hutchinson notes, "Bigger congregations meant bigger churches meant, quite often, that we stopped looking for the millennium and started building for it."[18] This growth and shift in ecclesiology has also impacted the wider mission of the Australian Pentecostal movement. Instead of identifying themselves as 'Hadassah' (the humble Hebrew flower), Pentecostals in Australia began to see themselves as agents of change and transformation within the structures of society and government—i.e., as "Esther" (the grand Gentile goddess). No longer waiting for the *parousia*, the victorious life could be experienced here and now. The Diaspora dream of Esther is active today, with Pentecostals too becoming a key influencer in the land as we navigate our way from the margins of society to the centre. The promise is that Pentecostals today can fulfil the Diaspora dream of functioning in positions of influence, which is to be desired by both Pentecostal and non-Pentecostal alike.

While this aspiration to move from exile to being strategically located in the centre has led to some positive outcomes, such as the planning and development of institutional structures, it has come packaged in the wrapping of "triumphalism." This feeling is reflected in an official statement, published in 2009, outlining the values of the Assemblies of God in Australia (AGA); it includes this assertion:

---

[18]Hutchinson, Mark, 'The New Thing God Is Doing: The Charismatic Renewal and Classical Pentecostalism,' *Australiasian Pentecostal Studies*, Vol. 1, March 1998, 5-21.

Life is meant to be lived as an increasing adventure in prosperity. God's intention is to prosper the righteous so that they can demonstrate the power of His Kingdom on earth. Prosperity is not an option but a mandate and responsibility given to all who believe in the authority of the name of Jesus. We are called to show forth the wonders of His increasing Kingdom, and this clearly requires an increasing measure of affluence so that we can have an increasing measure of influence.[19]

The sense of expectation, triumph, and focus on economic prosperity expressed in this statement captures the feeling of contemporary Pentecostalism in Australia as it drives to make God's kingdom established here on earth—not just in heaven! This paints a portrait of Diaspora life for the contemporary Pentecostal community—i.e., that living inside the margins is both successful and meaningful.[20] Part of this shift towards respectability, like Esther, has been the re-discovering or retrieval of our Wesleyan and Anabaptist heritage.[21] The surge of interest in the antecedents of Pentecostalism highlights that Pentecostals are no longer orphans. By retrieving our heritage, it adds legitimacy to our aspiration of influence and social inclusion. Like Esther, we are no longer marginal but stand at the centre of the community. Yet the question must be asked—What is the "cost" of this shift of Pentecostalism from the margins to the centre?

---

[19](http://www.aog.org.au/AboutUs/KeyValues/LovePeople/tabid/142/Default.aspx).
[20]Stern, 29. According to Stern, the message of Esther is not a defense of Diaspora living but rather "a comic critique of it" (p.31). Yet, this anti-reading still places the narrative in the setting of Diaspora.
[21]See for example, Matthew Clark, "An Investigation into the Nature of a Viable Pentecostal Hermeneutic," Thesis for D Th, Pretoria: Unisa; (1997) and Walter J. Hollenweger, "The Critical Tradition of Pentecostalism," *Journal of Pentecostal Theology*, vol. 1, (1992), 7-17.

The Transformation of Pentecostalism

Like Esther, Pentecostals in Australia see themselves as agents of change and transformation by functioning within the centre of the "world" or earthly kingdom in which we exist. We see opportunities to shine as "stars" like Queen Esther (and perhaps even like Ishtar) as being a God-given opportunity. In this approach, we consider every type of work, whether secular or religious, to be both successful and meaningful. Like Queen Esther and Mordecai, each has a calling and vocation, even if that vocation is in the court of the Gentile king. But what if that calling is to be placed in the philosophical harem of our contemporary academy? Or what if that vocation is to write edicts that promote the welfare of one group over another? The lines between the secular and the sacred have blurred. This is not necessarily negative, as Pentecostals begin to engage with the broader issues of the culture and politics of our societies and leave behind the siege mentality. However, as we navigate the "Empire," this blurring has the potential for us to lose our way and forget our mission. As Volf notes, "If one can describe with Luther the 'lifting of a single straw' as a 'completely divine' work, there is no reason why one should not be able to ascribe the same attribute to the most degrading types of work in industrial societies in which the human person is reduced to 'a mere automaton, a wooden man.'"[22]

Using the position of influence to further our own group, ideologies, or even theologies at the expense of others is contrary to the wisdom of the Gospel. It can lead us to endorse callings and vocations that undermine the dignity of humanity created in the image of God for the goal of influence. In this sense, there is potential for the vehicle to become the goal—i.e., that Pentecostals become so mesmerised with our power and leadership that influence becomes the end goal. Thereby we forget this influence should have been merely a vehicle for justice and truth. For

---

[22]Miroslav Volf, "Human Work, Divine Spirit, and New Creation: Towards a Pneumatological Understanding of Work," *Pneuma*, Fall 1987, 173-193.

the contemporary Pentecostal community navigating life in the Empire of secular humanism (and thus embracing the "star" of Esther), we should not forget that we are also the "myrtle" of Hadassah—a branch of the tree of Christ that should bring restoration and transformation of the desert (or place of exile) from thorns to flourishing.

GIDEON AND THE ANGEL OF THE LORD: AN ANTHROPOLOGICAL PERSPECTIVE ON JUDGES 6:11-40

by Dave Johnson

Introduction

The story of Gideon is set in the time of the judges sometime after the conquest of Israel.[1] During this period, the "nation" of Israel could best be described as a loose federation of tribes bound together by a shared ethnicity and, more importantly, under a covenant with *Yahweh* as their God and patron. Despite major differences in the religious practices of Israel and the Canaanite nations that surrounded them, there were also substantial cultural and worldview similarities.[2] Ramsay notes, "there was so much exchange of cultural influences between Israel and its neighbours on all sides of its tiny territory."[3] Understanding the cultural background is critical to understanding the biblical text and will help avoid importing foreign theological significance to some of the text's features.

The purpose of this essay is to understand the story of Gideon as he might have understood it and to make application to the broader Asian

---

[1] W.F. Albright dates the time of Gideon in the 11th century BC. William F. Albright, *Archaeology and the Religion of Israel*, Garden City, NY: Doubleday & Company, Inc., 1969, 109.
[2] John Walton, Victor H. Matthews, and Mark W. Chavalas, *The Bible Background Commentary: The Old Testament*, Downer's Grove, IL: InterVarsity Press, 2000, 11.
[3] Ramsay, *Yahweh and the Gods of Canaan: A Historical Analysis of Two Contrasting Faiths*. Winona Lake, IN: Eisenbrauns, n.d., 207.

context today.⁴ The tools of cultural anthropology used will specifically relate to patron-client relationships and the animistic practices prevalent in Palestine at the time. Focus will also be given to the animistic worldview that is revealed in the story. However, the story of the battle and Gideon's ungodly lifestyle that followed, as well as the story of Abimelech which forms part of the Gideon narrative (chaps. 7-8), is beyond the scope of this essay due to space limitations.

While Israel had been in the Promised Land for only a short time, there was already growing evidence of compromise and syncretism with the religious practices of the Canaanites who had not yet been driven out of the land. Specifically, there is plenty of evidence of Baalism, which according to L'Heureux, originated in the Middle Euphrates region of what is now Syria, north of Israel.⁵ Baalism was most likely carried by traders traveling through Canaan. It was already in the land and would later rise to become a state religion in the northern kingdom of Ahab and Jezebel.

Baalism, like animistic religions in the Ancient Near East (ANE) and the modern world, dealt with the daily affairs of life such as weather, crops, etc. It was not so concerned with issues such as sin, salvation, and eternal judgment. Sacrifices were made to appease the local Baals, to ensure a good harvest without pestilence, and to avoid natural disasters. Also, the images of the Baals served as a reminder to the people, who were largely illiterate, that the gods were watching over them, so its appeal is understandable. Yahwehism, with its prohibitions of images, was unique among the religions of ancient Mesopotamia.

Gorospe accurately points out that this does not mean that the Israelites abandoned Yahweh when they turned to Baalism. However, he

---

⁴While I am well aware that using the term "Asian context" in the singular can lead to over generalization to the point of being inaccurate, the wide practice of animism (even within the major religions) in Asia allow for the use of the singular term here.

⁵Conrad E. L'Heureux, *Rank Among the Canaanite Gods El, Ba'al and the Repha'im*, Harvard Semitic Monographs No. 21, ed. Frank Moore Cross, (Missoula, MT: Scholar's Press, 1979), 13.

was marginalized as their Lord and patron.[6] Indeed, the flexible nature of an animistic worldview meant that the Israelites, who had come of age as a nation in polytheistic Egypt, would not necessarily see any contradiction between these two religious systems. Moreover, as Gorospe notes, "Israel projects onto Yahweh the way it regards its idols—as gods to be appeased and manipulated in order to bless one's plans and family. In this way, God is not only marginalized but also domesticated and shamed."[7] In light of Yahweh's covenant relationship with Israel, with blessings and curses clearly stipulated in Deuteronomy 28, one is not left to wonder why Yahweh's anger was kindled against his people.

Setting

L.C. Wood notes that the exact location of Ophrah is not certain. It was located in the half-tribe of Manasseh that settled on the west side of the Jordan, north of the territory of Ephraim, which explains Gideon's interaction with the Ephraimites in 7:24-8:21.[8] Due to the topography of the land, many battles in Israel's history took place in this part of the country. accessible to their enemies both from the west and the east. At least part of the battle passed through Succoth, not far west of the Jordan.

The Midianites were descendants of Midian, a son of Abraham by his second wife, Keturah. R. L. Allen notes that they were not, however, part of the covenant of Israel and, with the exception of Jethro's kindness to Moses, were hostile to Israel.[9] The notation that they were in association with the peoples of the east suggests that they may have migrated from the Sinai Peninsula in the time of Jethro, to somewhere east of Moab by the time of Gideon. Allen, perhaps a bit pejoratively, goes on to note that as desert nomads, their lifestyle focused on "trading,

---

[6]Athena E. Gorospe, *Judges*, Asia Bible Commentary Series, ed. Frederico Villanueva, (Carlisle, UK: Langham Global Library, 2016), Kindle loc. 474.

[7]Gorospe and Ringma, Kindle loc. 469.

[8]L.C. Wood, "Ophrah," in *The Zondervan Pictorial Encyclopedia of the Bible*, ed., Merrill C. Tenney, vol. 4, 541-2, (Grand Rapids: Zondervan, 1976), 541.

[9]R. L. Allen, "Midian, Midanites," in *The Zondervan Pictorial Encyclopedia of the Bible*, ed., Merrill C. Tenney, vol. 4, 220-3, (Grand Rapids: Zondervan, 1976), 222.

travelling, and troubling others."¹⁰ In this case, however, their "troubling others" was permitted by Yahweh because the Israelites, who *were* the children of the covenant, were not adhering to the covenant (Judges 6:1). The Israelites' disobedience and Midian's "troubling" form the backdrop to Gideon's divine encounter.

Gideon and the Angel (6:11-24)

In the Bible, angels were frequently used by God to deliver messages to people on his behalf. K. Lawson Younger posits that this angel is a theophany, an appearance by God himself.¹¹ While Younger is not alone in this interpretation, which certainly has merit, this may not be the case here. Walton, Matthews and Chavalas note that heads of state in the ancient world rarely communicate directly, requiring the use of intermediaries, who were fully invested with the power and authority of the one they represented.¹² The use of an intermediary was not limited to communication between equals. In hierarchal societies, intermediaries are also used to communicate with those of higher or lower status.

The Terebinth Tree

The author notes that the angel sat under "the terebinth tree at Ophrah,"¹³ implying that this tree was well known to his original readers. In an animistic worldview, geographical locations such as mountains, caves, and in some cases, trees, were known to be portals where one might have contact with the supernatural world. Trent Butler may be correct that Gideon selected this spot for threshing his wheat since no

---

¹⁰Ibid.

¹¹K. Lawson Younger, *Judges, Ruth,* NIV Application Commentary, Grand Rapids: Zondervan, Kindle loc. 3540.

¹²Walton, Matthews and Chavalas, 253.

¹³All Scripture references in this article are taken from the English Standard Version unless otherwise noted.

one would have expected that kind of activity in a place known to be used for religious purposes.[14]

The terebinth tree, which the King James Version and New International Version render as "oak," was well known in ancient Palestine as one of those portals to the supernatural realm (i.e. Hosea 4:12,13). In Genesis 12:6-7, God appeared to Abraham under the terebinth at Shechem to repeat his covenant promises; Abraham responded by building an altar there. In Genesis 13:18, Abraham pitched his tent under a terebinth tree and built an altar to the Lord. In 18:1, the Lord appeared to him there. In Genesis 35:4, Jacob buried the idols of his company under a terebinth. That God would speak to Gideon under this tree suggests God's willingness to communicate with humanity within their cultural framework. Yahweh, however, was not the only deity worshiped under these trees. Butler notes that it was a common place to erect Baal shrines, which appears to be the case here, as well as in Gen 35:4; Ezek.6:13; and Hosea 4:13, (cf. I Kgs 13:14; I Chr 10:12).[15] This suggests that worshipers of Baal and Yahweh shared many aspects of the same worldview.

Salutation and Response

The salutation to Gideon is one of honor ascribed by God, not one earned by Gideon at this point. The background cultures of the Old Testament (OT), as well as Israel itself, were honor/shame cultures, as are Asian cultures today. Jerome Neyrey writes that honor was "the worth or value of persons both in their eyes and in the eyes of their village, neighborhood, or society. . . . The critical item is the public nature of respect and reputation."[16] Brown defines shame as "the intensely

---

[14]Trent C. Butler, *Judges*, Word Biblical Commentary 8, (Grand Rapids: Zondervan, 2009), 201.
[15]Butler, 201.
[16]Jerome H. Neyrey, *Honor and Shame in the Gospel of Matthew*, (Louisville, Ky: Westminster John Knox Press, 1998), 15. Quoted in Warner Mischke, *The Global Gospel: Achieving Missional Impact in Our Multicultural World*, (Scottsdale, AZ: Mission One Resources, 2015)**, 38.**

painful feeling or experience of believing that we are flawed and therefore unworthy of love and belonging . . . [including] the fear of disconnection."[17] As we will see in this text, the concept of shame and honor is not limited to human relationships.

The angel's statement that God is with Gideon contrasts with the reality that Gideon was hiding what he was doing from the pagan Midianites, begging the question that Gideon asks in v13. Indeed, it appears that God is absent. Gideon's response indicates that he does not recognize the divine nature of his visitor and simply respectfully calls him אֲדֹנָי or "sir," suggesting that the angel appeared in human form.[18] Another indication that the visitor and Gideon are not quite connecting is that the angel uses the second person singular when he says that "the Lord is with you," (6:12) but Gideon responds in the first person plural in 6:13.[19] Apparently Gideon missed the angel's point that although God was with Gideon personally, he was not necessarily with the whole nation at this point.

Gideon assumed that if God was with the nation, he would display his power as Israel's patron. There are two possible reasons for Gideon's assumption: the most obvious is that God has done it before, of which Gideon reminds the angel. Gideon assumed that if God would protect previous generations he would do it for the current one. The second reason was not stated in the text and is, therefore, less obvious. Ancient Mesopotamian societies, like much of the non-western world today, were organized into patron-client relationships in which their deities were considered to be their patrons.[20] Paul Hiebert describes the roles of patrons and clients: "the patron is the master who assumes full

---

[17]Brene Brown, *Daring Greatly: How the Courage to be Vulnerable Transforms the Way We Live, Love, Parent, and Lead,* (New York: Gotham, 2012), 59, Quoted in Warner Mischke, *The Global Gospel: Achieving Missional Impact in Our Multicultural World,* (Scottsdale, AZ: Mission One Resources, 2015), 38-9.
[18]Gorospe, loc. 2197.
[19]Ibid.
[20]J. Andrew Dearman, *Religion and Culture in Ancient Israel,* Peabody, MA: Hendrickson Publishers, 1992, 16.

responsibility for the welfare of his clients, seeing to it that they have at least a minimum of food, shelter, and protection. In one sense, he is their father. Clients, in turn, must give their patron their full loyalty and labor."[21]

While Hiebert referred to human relationships, the same could be said of human relationships to deities in the cultures of the OT and in Asian history. For example, kings were often seen as priests. The Egyptian pharaohs were also considered to be descendants of the gods, much like the Japanese once held to be true of their emperor. Pharaoh's relationship to his people as that of a patron-client can be clearly seen in the story of Joseph. Pharaoh assumed the responsibility of caring for his people in a time of famine and the people responded with loyalty and servitude to him (Gen. 41:46-50; 47:18-20).

Yahweh fit this pattern and was perceived as the patron/ruler of Israel throughout the Old Testament. For this reason, Israel had no king in the period of the judges. Dearman notes that, like the deities of the surrounding Canaanite peoples, Yahweh spoke to the nation's patriarch, Abraham, and protected them from their enemies. Yahweh also dwelt among them above the mercy seat in the Holy of Holies in the Mosiac tabernacle at Shiloh.[22] When the Israelites later demanded a king, they were rejecting God as both their king and their patron. Their pleas to other gods to receive blessings from them must also be seen as a rejection of Yahweh's patronage.

Gideon's question in 6:13 reveals one of two possibilities. First, he may have been ignorant of the blessings and curses of the covenant in Deuteronomy 28, which reflect a patron-client paradigm. Israel had clearly been disloyal to her patron in following other gods. The cry for help in 6:6 should be understood as a desire to restore the patron-client relationship because of the protection Yahweh offered, although

---

[21]Paul Hiebert, *Cultural Anthropology*, 2nd ed. (Grand Rapids: Baker Book House, 1983), 152.
[22]Dearman, 16.

Younger may also be correct in stating that the Israelites' cry contains "no hint at true repentance."[23] The other possibility is that, because Gideon would have had strong emotions and fears as one of the oppressed, he may not have clearly understood that Israel was under God's curse for not being loyal to their patron. Younger's statement that Gideon's comments reflect cynicism about God's treatment of the nation reflects another perspective for understanding his comments.[24]

In verse 14, the angel ignored Gideon's question and challenged him to rise to the occasion. What Gideon did not understand at this point was that by his own actions he would answer his own question, because God would work a miracle through him.

Again, Gideon's response revealed his worldview. He could not be "a mighty man of valor," nor a leader of any kind because he did not have the correct status. Patron-client societies have a clear social pecking order. Gideon's family was the least, from the tribe of Manasseh. As a half tribe, it was one of the smallest tribes in Israel. Gideon didn't have the status to do what was needed. Butler notes that Gideon may have understated the case since his father was a landowner and apparently one of the tribal leaders (6:25-32), thus giving Gideon some status, at least within his own clan.[25]

Gideon was clearly a client, not a patron, which may be precisely why God selected him. Throughout Scripture, God repeatedly honors and empowers those of low status (i.e., Moses in the wilderness, David, Mary, etc.). When God promised to be with him, it carried the understanding that this would give Gideon status, revealing that the social order was not inflexible and status could be gained or lost. Later, Gideon would be asked to be the ruler of his own people and some of the other tribes (Judges 8:22).

---

[23] Younger, loc. 3483.
[24] Ibid., loc. 3607.
[25] Butler, 203.

Gideon's request for a sign suggests that he was willing to consider trying to serve Israel's ultimate patron. Signs or omens to communicate the will of a deity or spirit are quite common in an animistic worldview. Gorospe sees this request for a sign as an indication that Gideon might now suspect that his visitor may not be human.[26]

The meal Gideon served appears unremarkable, as were the angel's instructions on how to serve it. Regarding motive, Gorospe suggests two possibilities. First, it could be a simple act of hospitality afforded to a guest. Second, it might be an offering of food to a deity.[27] The text is not clear and either seems possible, although I am not convinced that Gideon was yet aware of his visitor's divine status. When the angel vanished, however, Gideon's perception immediately changed. Now he was certain that God had visited him and he marveled that he was still alive. With a clearer vision of what was happening before him, Gideon likely grasped the fact that God was indeed with him, no matter that the circumstances may have suggested otherwise.

The Baal Shrine and the Asherah Pole (6:25-32)

William Albright states that Baal, like Yahweh was also seen as cosmic in power. Rather surprisingly, he also suggests that the collision between these two faiths would not dilute Yahweh's stature in Israel, although he admits that compromise would only result in Yahweh being regarded as a form of Baal.[28] While it is apparent from the OT that many Israelites reflected this point of view in their religious practices, Albright's position, in my opinion, conflicts with divine revelation. Throughout the OT, Yahweh repeatedly claimed to be the one and only God (i.e. Isaiah 45:22). Deborah's song from the same era as Gideon (Judges 5:1-31), while not denying the existence of other gods, clearly claimed Yahweh's superior power. Gideon's actions reflect the same

---

[26]Gorospe, loc. 2289.
[27]Ibid.
[28]Ramsay, *Archaeology*, 113.

attitude. To favorably compare any god with Yahweh would indeed dishonor Yahweh's name.

But there is another reason for this incompatibility. God would not tolerate allegiance to another patron. Tearing down the altar and the Asherah pole signified that God was asking Israel to visibly and concretely demonstrate that they were returning to Yahweh's patronage and renouncing that of Baal and the Asherah.

Frymer-Kensky observes that Asherah veneration came from Phoenicia.[29] White goes on to note that the worship of Asherah was fairly widespread throughout the ANE and would later rise to official cult status under Ahab and Phoenician-born Jezebel.[30] Asherah, a goddess of fertility in the Canaanite pantheon, was regarded as the consort of El, who was the top god among the Canaanite deities. White admits that other scholars consider her to be the consort of Baal or perhaps both El and Baal.[31] McCarter suggests that she may also have been a consort of Yahweh.[32] This blending of mythology and religious practices further reflects the worldview similarities of the various Canaanite peoples that Israel shared to some degree.

As Asherah was a goddess of fertility, Frymer-Kensky may be correct in saying, "The connection of Asherah to trees and groves and her location at altars hint that she represented, in some way, the natural world and its powers of regeneration."[33] There is much discussion among OT scholars as to whether the Asherah was a goddess, a cult symbol, or

---

[29]Tikva Frymer-Kensky, *In the Wake of the Goddess: Women, Culture, and the Biblical Transformation of Pagan Myth,* New York: (The Free Press, 1992), 156.

[30]White, "Asherah and the Asherim: Goddess or Cult Symbol?: Exploring the Biblical and Archaeological Evidence," *Bible History Daily,* www.biblicalarchaeology.org, 11/4/14 (accessed 19 June 2017).

[31]William F. Albright, *Yahweh,* 121, c.f. Ellen White, "Asherah and the Asherim: Goddess or Cult Symbol?: Exploring the Biblical and Archaeological Evidence," *Bible History Daily,* www.biblicalarchaeology.org, 11/4/14 (accessed 19 June 2017).

[32]P. Kyle McCarter, "The Religion of the Israelite Monarchy," in *Ancient Israelite Religion: Essays in Honor of Frank Moore Cross,* ed. Patrick Miller Jr., Paul Hanson, S. Dean McBride, (Philadelphia: Fortress Press, 1987), 143.

[33]Frymer-Kensky, *In the Wake,* 158.

both. Since the function of the Asherah is the same either way, and drew devotees away from Yahweh, these arguments need not be a concern.

LaRocca-Pitts notes that there is much debate as to whether the Asherah pole was a simple tree, or pole, or whether it reflected the goddess Asherah itself.[34] Theologically, however, this debate is beside the point. Throughout the Scriptures, God's aversion to idolatry is related to their function and the allegiance these idols call for, rather than their shape or size (cf. Is. 44:12-19; I Cor 8:4-6). Frymer-Kensky's statement that the "Asherah was not Yahweh's rival"[35] cannot be sustained in light of God's attitude toward it here. Yahweh himself clearly considered otherwise, both here and throughout the OT.

An Altar to Yahweh (6:23-7)

Missiologist Kevin Hovey notes that destroying an idol or shrine destroys its power over those who gave allegiance to it.[36] Doing so also publicly shamed Baal, something Gideon's townsmen clearly understood. They also feared Baal's retribution, and demanded that Gideon restore Baal's honor to avert the disaster they were certain Baal would cause.

It is important to note the angel's command to use the elements of the altar to Baal and the Asherah pole, in the altar to the Lord. In animism, symbolism is important. Destroying the Baal and Asherah shrines and using the elements to worship Yahweh conveyed Yahweh's superiority to, and power over, other gods.

Yahweh abhorred idolatry for many reasons, but in this case, the key issue of worshiping other gods was that the allegiance rightfully

---

[34]Elizabeth C. LaRocca-Pitts, *Of Wood and Stone: The Significance of Cultic Items in the Bible and Its Early Interpreters*, Harvard Semitic Monographs No. 61, ed. Peter Machinist, (Winona Lake, IN: Eisenbrauns, 2001.

[35]Frymer-Kensky, *In the Wake*, 217.

[36]I am not certain of when Hovey made this comment, but it was probably during a class lecture at the Asia Pacific Theology Seminary in 1995.

belonging to him was being given to Baal and Asherah. Framing this in the context of a patron-client relationship, Israel had reneged on its obligation to Yahweh and was serving another patron. In doing so, they had shamed Yahweh.

That Yahweh was jealous for his own honor is clear from Exodus 20:1-6; 34:14; Deuteronomy 4:24; and Ezek 39:25. This would have been well known to Gideon and his clansmen. Building an altar to the Lord in the place of the altar to Baal and the Asherah can be clearly seen as erasing Israel's shameful behavior while restoring God's honor as Israel's God and patron.

The Baal shrine may have belonged to Gideon's family. However, the reaction of the community, and Gideon's fear of them, suggest that more likely, the shrine belonged to the entire community with Gideon's father as the caretaker. The shrine belonging to more than a single individual would reflect the social nature of animistic practices and the group orientation of Israelite society. To break from the norm violated the patron-client relationship between the deity and the community. Not only was the deity shamed, this publicly shamed the entire community and threatened the social order as the deity might take vengeance on all of them.

That Gideon performed the deed at night comes as no surprise, given the level of allegiance that he and his townspeople had given to Baal, the communal nature of the shrine, and the widespread fear of Baal's revenge. Gorospe observes that persecution, especially of Christians, happens in many Asian societies whenever someone departs from the faith of the family or clan to embrace another religion.[37] Honor killing due to apostasy by conversion to another religion is practiced in some Asian societies today for the same reason that Gideon's community wanted his head.

Order could only be restored by dealing harshly with the offender. In many collectivistic societies, sin is seen more as a violation of the social

---

[37]Gorospe, loc 2367.

order, which in this case, included the relationship with their patron. That the community would demand that a father kill his own son suggests that they valued the honor of their community strongly, and feared the retribution of their deity, more than they valued the life of any individual.

Butler notes that Joash turns the narrative around by saying that Baal, not Gideon, is the guilty one.[38] However, shame, not guilt, is the issue here. Gideon has indeed shamed Baal, and by extension, his own family and community, by tearing down Baal's shrine. Joash's challenge to the community is that if Baal is who he claims to be, he can restore his own honor by taking revenge on Gideon.

As head of the clan, Joash was expected to keep his family in line with the community's expectations and was called upon to deal with this egregious offense. Joash's response was as brave as it is interesting. He might also be seen as avoiding his responsibility, but the fear of supernatural retribution would likely negate this. His comments could be understood to reflect a natural desire to see his son live, but they also suggest that he had his own doubts about Baal. Giving Gideon the name Jerubbaal also hinted that Joash was willing to admit to Baal's impotence.[39]

Note that there was no discussion here as to whether Baal really existed. His existence was taken for granted. Joash's challenge regarded his power. Then and now, the core issue in animistic practices is supernatural power. Joash's logic was difficult to refute. If Baal was god and a true patron, he could deal with Gideon himself and defend his own honor. Gideon, however, remained alive.

---

[38] Butler, *Judges*, 206.
[39] Ibid. Butler actually cites another scholar here but only give's the person's last name and the bibliographic reference is insufficient to identify the original source.

Gideon and Yahweh's Empowerment

By this time, Gideon had already begun to obey God's command by issuing a call to arms throughout the nearby Israelite tribes. The idea that "the Spirit of the Lord" clothed Gideon should be seen as anointing him for a specific purpose at a specific time and did not necessarily ascribe great spirituality to Gideon himself.[40] His actions in 8:1-32 revealed that his character left much to be desired. The issue of supernatural power again came into focus. The idea of a deity going to war with his people was widespread in the ANE. Indeed, tribes and nations would seek the assurance of their deity's aid before going on the offensive (i.e. Eze 21:21-3). That the other tribes recognized this "clothing" is evident from their response.[41] One of the duties of patron deities was to help in battle and thus bring honor to themselves. Restoring Yahweh's honor among his own people must be seen as part of the purpose for Gideon's empowerment.

Gideon and His Fleece (6:33-40)

Divination was widely practiced in the ANE and took many different forms. De Olmo Lete notes that "Canaanite religion exhibits a strong magical component completely integrated into the official cultic system. It's most striking expression, from the aspect of textual transmissions, is divination."[42] Like animistic practices in Asia today, divination was devoted to knowing the future. Through incantations and rituals, an individual tries to prevent future events from happening, direct them and, as a result, control them.[43]

---

[40]Ibid., 208.

[41]Daniel Block, "Will the Real Gideon Please Stand Up?" in *Journal of the Evangelical Theological Society*, 40, 1997, 353-66, 356 accessed www.ebscohost.com, August 28, 2017.

[42]Gregorio Del Olmo Lete, *Canaanite Religion According to the Liturgical Texts of Ugarit*, trans. Wilfred G.E. Watson, Winona Lake, IN: Eisenbrauns, 2004, 345.

[43]De Olmo Lete, 346 (accessed 19 June 2017).

Divination was expressly prohibited by Yahweh (i.e. Num. 22:7; Deut. 18:10; 2 Ki. 17:17; Eze. 12:24; 13:6-7; 21-3, etc.) when it focused on contact with spiritual forces other than Yahweh, or directed toward doing the will of the person or persons involved (I Sam. 28:3-25). In some cases, as I have noted elsewhere, a few forms of divination, such as the Urim and the Thummin and the interpretation of dreams (i.e. Gen. 41; Dan. 2:1-45) were clearly sanctioned, or at least allowed, by Yahweh to accomplish his purposes.[44] The key difference in usage, or permission, was when Yahweh himself was the at the heart of the matter and used these methods to communicate his will in a cultural way that humans would understand. Such was the case with Gideon. In contrast, animism is anthropocentric, not theocentric.

Gideon's fleece, like the Urim and the Thummin, was a mechanical form of divination that operated in a binary matter, answering only yes or no.[45] Walton, Matthews, and Chavalas compare Gideon's actions to that of Eliezer with Rebekah (Genesis 24:14) and the Philistines in sending the Ark of the Covenant back to Israel (I Samuel 6:7-9). Unlike the divinatory practices of his Canaanite neighbors and those still prevalent in Asia, Gideon only tried to discern the will of God for the future. He did not try to direct or control it. This distinction is important as it indicates that Gideon was trying to follow Yahweh, not control him.

Butler notes numerous scholars that fault Gideon for doing this, suggesting that he was lacking in faith, etc.[46] I see this a bit differently. Given the capricious nature of the gods of the Canaanite pantheon, typical of animistic thinking then and now, I suggest that he may have perceived the God of Israel in a similar manner and wanted to make sure that Yahweh had not changed his mind.[47] Furthermore, his actions are understandable, considering he was about to place men in harm's way.

---

[44]Dave Johnson, *Theology in Context: A Case Study in the Philippines*, (Baguio City, Philippines: APTS Press, 2013, 100-101.
[45]Walton, Matthews and Chavalas, 255.
[46]Butler, 210.
[47]Walton, Matthews and Chavalas, 255.

Since consulting the Urim and the Thummin would have required Gideon to go to the high priest, for which there was no time, Gideon simply used what he had available. After the fleece, Gideon showed no further hesitation in carrying out God's command.

There is no hint in the narrative that Gideon's actions met with Yahweh's disapproval. He responded in a way that gave Gideon the confidence to move forward, which he promptly did. Yahweh brought about a great victory and Yahweh's honor was restored, at least for a time.

Application in Asian Contexts

Patron-client relationships in both the natural and supernatural realms are prevalent throughout Asia. In the Philippines, every town has a patron saint that is believed to deliver the community from disaster and do a multitude of other things. People respond by paying homage through an annual festival, which includes special masses in honor of the saint and may also include a procession throughout the community.

Some Hindu festivals honor various Hindu deities.[48] Folk Buddhist festivals and holidays honoring the Buddha or the ancestors follow the same pattern of patron-client thinking.[49] Phil Parshall notes a number of folk Islamic practices that also fit a patron-client paradigm.[50] While it must be noted that the patron saints (including the Virgin Mary) in the Philippines and the ancestors in folk Buddhism and Islamic traditions are not considered deities, their function is much the same.

Strong family ties and group-oriented societies are the norm in societies honoring patron-client relationships. Breaking tradition to embrace the gospel of Jesus Christ is often seen as dishonoring the family and upsetting the social order. This may also threaten an individual's identity and place in the family or community. Persecutions, including being ostracized from the community, and even being killed, are often

---

[48]http://www.religionfacts.com/hinduism/holidays, (accessed August 25, 2017).
[49]Ibid.
[50]Phil Parshall, *Bridges to Islam*, (Grand Rapids: Baker Book House, 1985), 73-76.

the result. In Gideon's case, God intervened. In many, many other cases, however, believers suffer for Jesus' name just like the heroes of the faith in Hebrews 11:32-38.

In the both the ANE and in modern Asia, animistic practices dominate the religious landscape, usually operating under a thin veneer of Islam, Buddhism, Hinduism and, to some extent, Christianity. This clearly suggests that animism is at home in more than one religious system, even though folk practices are at odds with formal doctrine.[51] As they were in Gideon's day, these practices remain heavily anthropocentric, dealing with issues of daily life such the weather, romance, and a multitude of other things. They focus on gaining, using, and maintaining supernatural power from demonic forces in rebellion against God.

Biblical Response to Animism

While a complete discussion on this subject would fill several volumes, some critical points can be made. Since animistic practices in Asia are woven deeply into the cultural fabric of Asian societies, care must be taken to avoid two extremes. On one hand, Hiebert, Shaw, and Tinou adamantly claim that ignoring the issues will lead to syncretism.[52] On the other hand, attempting to stamp out such practices without dealing with the worldview issues that lie beneath them, also leads to syncretism or "split-level Christianity."[53] Unfortunately, for reasons beyond the scope of this essay, many western missionaries working in

---

[51] Catholics in the Philippines, which make up about 80% of the population, are heavily involved in folk religious practices. The most honest description of Catholicism here is to describe it as Cristo-paganism. Also, Peram Chin, one of my DMin students from Myanmar, related how some in the mostly Christian tribal groups still participate in Buddhist festivals.

[52] Paul Hiebert, R. Daniel Shaw and Tite Tienou, *Understanding Folk Religion: A Christian Response to Popular Beliefs and Practices*, (Grand Rapids: Baker Book House, 1999), 369.

[53] Ibid.

Asia and some Asian pastors themselves, have fallen into both extremes.[54]

The best response to animistic practices is described by Hiebert as "critical contextualization."[55] For Hiebert, this involves several steps. The first step calls for exegeting the culture by knowing the traditional religious practices and why people do them. The second step calls for exegeting the Scripture, including the pagan backgrounds of both the OT and New Testament. In this step, Hiebert argues that theology, anthropology, and linguistics have much to offer. Finally, the people involved must critically evaluate their old customs in light of the Scripture and get rid of the practices that contradict Scripture. Finally, they can institute new rituals and customs that provide them opportunities to worship the Lord within their own context.[56]

The Gideon narrative is an excellent case in point. Sacrificing to a deity was nothing new among the Canaanites. The distinction was that Gideon and the Israelites were to offer sacrifices to the Lord. The same was true with Gideon's fleece. While I find no evidence that the Canaanites used sheep's skins in their divinatory practices, the idea of using a material item, or animal parts, to consult a deity was quite common (Eze. 21:21) in the ANE. The difference with Gideon was not in what he did, but in what his purpose was—to reconfirm the will of God. In both of his actions, God was the focus of his actions, not Baal. In

---

[54]For an excellent discussion on why western missionaries fail to deal well with animistic issues, see Paul Hiebert's influential article "The Flaw of the Excluded Middle," *Missiology* 10 no. 1 (January, 1982): 35-47. In my observation, some Filipino pastors don't deal with these issues because some Filipinos are embarrassed to admit that these things go on because they feel it makes them sound like uneducated, country bumpkins. In other cases, especially for Asians who have been educated in the West, they appear to have taken on western theological orientations that do not teach them how to deal with these issues. At a recent theological consultation I attended in Malang, Indonesia, some attendees noted that Asian scholars have not yet learned how to exegete culture.

[55]Paul Hiebert, *Anthropological Reflections on Missiological Issues*, (Grand Rapids: Baker Books, 1994), 88.

[56]Ibid., 88-91.

the case of the altar, Gideon's action was commanded by God. In the fleece, God responded to Gideon's request with no indication of disfavor.

Conclusion

This essay began with the stated goal of looking at part of the story of Gideon using the tools of cultural anthropology and seeking to understand the events as he himself might have done, in order to make broader application to Asia today. The impact of significant cultural values like shame and honor and patron-client relationships in both the OT and modern Asia, with implications for human relationships to one another, and to the supernatural, have been demonstrated here. The rejection of animistic worldviews, then and now, demonstrates Yahweh's aversion to allegiance to anything other than himself. Above all, the relevance and the lesson of the story of Gideon and its call to serve Yahweh alone, speak loudly in Asian contexts today.

Tragedy of Spirit-Empowered Heroes: A Close Look at Samson and Saul[1]

by Wonsuk Ma

Introduction

The emergence and growth of Pentecostal and charismatic Christianity are often regarded as contributing significantly to making the twentieth century a "surprise Christian century." Among many positive contributions of the Pentecostal-Charismatic movements today, however, bright charismatic "stars" have fallen on moral grounds and have punctuated like deep scars its otherwise glowing face. The problem is, this grave failure is not limited to the "stars" such as megachurch pastors and televangelists. A lax attitude is also observed among less-than-starry leaders in the Pentecostal-Charismatic world. Even if the rate of failure is comparable to that of other leaders, it is still a disturbing reality. Why are people who experience the presence of the Holy Spirit no different from those who do not share the same experience? If "empowerment for service" is the main purpose of such spiritual encounters, then would it not be unfair for these leaders to be used as a machine or tool for specific purposes and then thrown away the next moment? If the Holy Spirit is not a force but a person, doesn't this create a serious theological dilemma? This rather disturbing question has

---

[1] This study, originally prepared for this volume, was published under the same title in *Spiritus: ORU Journal of Theology* 2:1&2 (2017) with the permission of the volume editor(s).

led me to notice similar failures among the Spirit-empowered heroes of old.

Samson and Saul are two leaders who rank the first and second places on the leaderboard of Spirit-endued charismatic leaders in the Old Testament. Samson records four references to the coming of the Spirit, all positive (Judg 13:25; 14:6, 19; 15:14). On the other hand, Saul has a whopping ten references, but five of them are to "the evil spirit (from God)" (1 Sam 16:15, 16, 23; 18:10; 19:9).[2] Then two refers to the departure of God's Spirit (1 Sam 16:15) and the Spirit's work to immobilize him (19:23). These leave only three references (1 Sam 10:6, 10; 11:6). My immediate inquiry is this: is there any textual evidence to suggest the presence of the Spirit beyond the empowerment of heroes? I decided to limit my search to historical Spirit-empowered heroes, or charismatic leaders, as the future figures such as the ideal king in Isa 11 and the Servant in Isa 42 would represent an ideal type of Spirit-empowered leader(s).

If the Spirit would affect the inner being of the hero, it would have to be in a private setting. Such a case would also be expected at the beginning of the hero's career rather than later. And references then would employ language which would suggest the internal and private effect of the Spirit. In both heroes, such passages are found: Judg 13 and 1 Sam 10. The inclusion of these passages is made possible due to the multiple references by Samson and Saul to the coming of God's Spirit. Understandably, almost no attention will be given to the famous passages which describe their exploits of the enemies. At the same time, this study faces a serious challenge: we are talking about only a few passages, and sometimes the meaning of certain terms is uncertain. This challenge will make it almost impossible to investigate the process and nature of the Spirit's work on the values, spirituality, and morality of a person. In the end, there may be no conclusive outcome.

---

[2]My count is among historical figures, excluding the "Servant," for example, with a good number of references to the Spirit of God in the book of Isaiah.

This study, therefore, will take a close look at the two passages and capture any notion of the Spirit's internal work within the heroes. The study concludes with any implications to the contemporary Christian life, especially applicable to Pentecostal-Charismatic believers.

> Judges 13:24–25
> The woman bore a son, and named him Samson. The boy grew, and the Lord blessed him. The spirit of the Lord began to stir him in Mahaneh-dan, between Zorah and Eshtaol.[3]

The book is structured by what is often called the repetition of a "theological cycle." Israel deserted its God and resorted to other gods. God "gave" Israel to an oppressive enemy hand, Israel sought God in repentance, then God prepared a deliverer (e.g., Judg 2:10–16). This destitute state of the loosely organized tribal alliance is regularly attributed to the lack of a central rule, or king: "In those days there was no king in Israel; all the people did what was right in their own eyes" (Judg 17:6; also 18:1; 19:1; 21:25). In a way, the whole book prepares for the emergence of an Israelite monarchy. Samson is the last judge to be recorded. At the conclusion of the previous judges (in this case, Jephthah followed by three others, Judg 12), strangely the normal theological cycle simply disappears. Conspicuously lacking is the repentance element.[4] Instead, Samson's miraculous birth account is introduced.

The birth of a hero has a certain literary pattern and Samson's case shares some of its features, including the appearance of God's messenger; pregnancy after an extended period of barrenness; childbirth through God's intervention; restrictions imposed on the mother, as well as on the child; and above all, God's special plan for the new hero. The chapter also serves to present Samson's call to a judgeship. This cascading of

---

[3] All the scriptural quotes are from New Revised Standard Version.
[4] David G. Firth, "The Spirit and Leadership: Testimony, Empowerment and Purpose," in David G. Firth and Paul D. Wegner (eds.), *Presence, Power and Promise: The Role of the Spirit of God in the Old Testament* (Nottingham: Apollos, 2010), 274.

extraordinary elements surrounding his birth builds a strong sense of expectation.⁵ After all, God gave him a "sound mind and a strong body as he grew to maturity."⁶ Now, on what basis commentator Herbert Wolf assumes that Samson is endowed with a "sound mind" is uncertain.

Judges 13:25 records the fulfillment of God's promise of a child and his early years. In this brief statement, God's blessing is upon him. In his growing years, he experiences God's Spirit. In referring to the coming of the Spirit upon Samson, the author of Judges employs a strange word instead of the stereotypical verb, צָלַח which is quite frequently used in association with the coming of the Spirit. In fact, in all the subsequent occasions when the Spirit of God comes upon Samson, the author employs this common verb. In this first incident of the Spirit upon him, there is a strong sense that the context is in a private setting. No reference is made to anyone else being present when this occurred. A close look at this experience needs to take two components of the text into account: the verb and its effect, and the significance of the locations or the lack thereof.

The Verb פָּעַם

Determining the exact meaning of the verb פָּעַם also poses a challenge. Its verbal form occurs only five times in the Old Testament: once in qal or piel form (in the present verse), three times in niphal (Gen 41:8; Ps 77:4; Dan 2:3) and once in hithpael form (Dan 2:1).⁷ Nonetheless, its usages are consistent: four of the five times, the term is used with "spirit": once with that of Yahweh, and the others with human spirits. When it is used in relation to the human spirit, the persons are actively influenced or "stirred," in each case by dreams. Pharaoh's spirit

---

⁵Trent C. Butler, *Judges*, Word Biblical Commentary (Nashville, TN: Thomas Nelson, 2009), 331.
⁶Herbert Wolf, "Judges," in *Deuteronomy, Joshua, Judges, Ruth, 1, 2 Samuel*, Expository Bible Commentary 3 (Grand Rapids, MI: Zondervan, 1992), 464.
⁷M. Sæbø, "פָּעַם," *Theological Dictionary of the Old Testament*, vol. 12 (Grand Rapids, MI: Eerdmans, 2003), 43.

was disturbed by dreams (Gen 41:8), and so was Nebuchadnezzar's (Dan 2:1, 3). In these cases, the verb can denote the emotional state of the persons, such as "disturbed" or "agitated."[8] But this can also refer to a more active state, such as "moved, anxious, rest-less" [sic] to learn the meaning of the dream.[9]

Of course, Samson's encounter is with God's Spirit and its effect, and, one may argue, it can be different from other cases. Here are several translations: "to stir" (NIV, NRSV), "to move [him] at times" (KJV), "to drive [him] hard,"[10] "to arouse,"[11] "to direct,"[12] or simply "to accompany" (LXX). Drawing from the passages associated with dreams, a generally disturbing or restless state of mind may be agreed on. Although a dream and God's Spirit may be quite different, both were considered by ancient minds to belong to the spiritual realm. For this reason, David Firth argues that the Spirit's stirring was "in directions he would not have chosen."[13] Wolf contends, along this same line, that the intention of the stirring was for Samson to deliver his people from the Philistine oppression.[14]

However, I would like to argue that this encounter tends to point to a more internal and personal nature of the Spirit's work. First, unlike the subsequent coming of the Spirit upon Samson, there is neither an enemy present nor imminent danger. In fact, this experience may have taken place away from people (as seen below). Secondly, despite its brevity, this is part of the record of his initial "call." In this context, the coming of the Spirit serves to affirm God's call upon the hero, not to empower for a

---

[8]John Gray, *Joshua, Judges, Ruth*, New Century Bible Commentary (Grand Rapids, MI: Eerdmans, 1986), 327.
[9]Sæbø, "פעם," 46.
[10]James D. Martin, *The Book of Judges* (Cambridge: Cambridge University Press, 1975), 151.
[11]Robert G. Boling, *Judges: Introduction, Translation and Commentary*, Anchor Bible (Garden City, NY: Doubleday, 1975), 226.
[12]Firth, "The Spirit and Leadership," 275.
[13]David Firth, "Historical Books," in Trevor J. Burke and Keith Warrington (eds.), *A Biblical Theology of the Holy Spirit* (London: SPCK, 2014), 17.
[14]Wolf, "Judges," 465.

military campaign. In the case of Saul, after his initial encounter with the Spirit in a private setting in this passage, the empowering nature of the Spirit took place subsequently in 1 Sam 11. In this case, the Spirit's presence and its effect served as a sign of God's call to Samson. Thirdly, related to the preceding point, the result of the Spirit's coming in this passage does not indicate anything public, such as a military feat as seen in the subsequent record. Yes, there is no record of the effect whatsoever. Nonetheless, the absence of any publicly displayed action points to the private nature of this experience. Consequently, Wolf's suggestion may have gone beyond the warrant of the text.

Places

In view of the extremely insufficient textual evidence, would the place named found in the same verse help us towards the establishment of the internal work of the Spirit? Ancient place names are often hard to identify with accuracy. Mahaneh-dan is a region which includes Zorah and Eshtaol. Zorah is identified as Samson's hometown (13:2). Although the exact location of Eshtaol cannot be established, these two locations were customarily used to identify the extent of the Danite territory. For this reason, these two places appear as a pair, except in 13:2. In the Samson narratives, the Spirit "stirred" him "between Zorah and Eshtaol," and he was later buried "between Zorah and Eshtaol" (16:31). Although several commentators believe that, unlike Zorah, Eshtaol was an area with no population,[15] the usage in ch. 18 does not support this. In all three references, "men from Zorah and Eshtaol" went out to spy a new land (18:2, cf. 18:8). Later, six hundred men from these two places went out to fight for the land (18:11). Moreover, the passages are clear that these men from the two locations were "all the Danites" (18:2, 11).

---

[15]Trent C. Butler, *Judges*, Word Biblical Commentary (Nashville, TN: Thomas Nelson, 2009), 331.

It is evident that Danites at this time were in a nomadic state, before moving to the northeast. That is why their oppressors were Philistines, while ch. 18 records their attempt to explore a new territory. Zorah and Eshtaol served as the boundary markers as well as the major towns of the Danite territory. However, there seemed to be an inhabited area between these two major locations, and this is where Samson's references took place. Hence, the first experience of Samson with the Spirit is likely intended to be private due to its location and its circumstance.

Summary

The nature of the internal effect is not apparent beyond any textual evidence. However, one thing is clear: This experience is meant to remind Samson of his life calling and God's lordship. The "stirring" or "agitating" work of the Spirit can easily be perceived as challenging his comfort zone. Combined with God's careful endowment of life's gifts, including his birth itself, he then is truly expected to be a godly hero. Thus, it is not too farfetched to argue for the transformative work of the Spirit at this stage, either in attitude, spiritual and contextual awareness, his life calling or mission, etc.

Butler is right, as are others, that the coming of the Spirit is not an approval of his spiritual condition. But I am not sure if I can completely agree with him that the Spirit does not "fill him with an inner spirituality."[16] Yes, the text does not represent a "transformation" of Samson by the Spirit.[17] However, the current discussion suggests at least the possibility of the inner-working of the Spirit in Samson as he grew. Elsewhere, the work of the Spirit in inner transformation is observed. For example, in Gideon's case, Firth argues that he was transformed from a "fearful" to a "wise and courageous" leader, although this did not occur

---

[16]Ibid., 330.
[17]R. G. Bowman, "Narrative Criticism of Judges," in G. A. Yee (ed.), *Judges and Method: New Approaches in Biblical Studies*, 2nd ed. (Minneapolis: Fortress, 2007), 38–39.

immediately after his experience of the Spirit.[18] It was through the radical victory with a small army which can only be attributed to divine work (Judg 7:2).

Then, a lesson drawn by several scholars is worth noting. In spite of God's extraordinary preparation of gifts, Samson failed in character development, [19] and his whole life is marked by tragedy.[20] The victories he achieved through the manifestation of his military and physical prowess by the Spirit just amount to "saving his own neck."[21] Furthermore, some threats he had to face were of his own making!

What then was the Spirit doing in the making of this young hero? As with many endowed gifts, I may argue, the coming of the Spirit was to enhance God's giftedness in him and to challenge him with the encounter of God's reality to contribute to the process of his character development. Then, Bowman is absolutely right: "It appears that divine power is constrained by the exercise of human freedom. Divine success appears contingent upon an appropriate human response."[22]

1 Samuel 10:6–7, 9

[6]Then the spirit of the Lord will possess you, and you will be in a prophetic frenzy along with them and be turned into a different person. [7]Now when these signs meet you, do whatever you see fit to do, for God is with you. [9]As he turned away to leave Samuel, God gave him another heart; and all these signs were fulfilled that day.

This passage records the long process of Saul's accession to kingship.

---

[18]Firth, "Historical Books," 16.
[19]J. C. Exum and J. W. Wheedbee, "Isaac, Samson, and Saul: Reflections on the Comic and Tragic Visions," in P.R. House (ed.), *Beyond Form Criticism: Essays in Old Testament Literary Criticism* (Winona Lake, IN: Eisenbrauns, 1992), 302.
[20]Wolf, "Judges," 465.
[21]Wonsuk Ma, "The Empowerment of the Spirit of God in Luke-Acts: An Old Testament Perspective," in Wonsuk Ma and Robert P. Menzies (eds.), *The Spirit and Spirituality: Essays in Honour of Russell P. Spittler* (London: T & T Clark, 2004), 31.
[22]Bowman, "Narrative Criticism of Judges," 38–39.

After the book of Judges' portrayal of longing for the appearance of a king in Israel, the books of Samuel picture a rather troubling origin of the monarchy. Samuel, who combined the offices of prophet and priest, practically ruled the nation in continuation of the judge tradition. The people's demand for a king was caused by the misbehaviors of Samuel's sons (1 Sam 8:5), and God's consent to the demand marks a new era. It is natural, though, to expect that the new leader, now called נָגִיד, would follow the pattern of the judges. And the divine appointment accompanied by the coming of God's Spirit is the core of the rise of God's chosen leader. In an extremely private and even secretive circumstance, Saul was now anointed by Samuel into kingship. The passage depicts in great detail a part of the third sign, the experience with the Spirit, which the prophet promised to validate this election.

Before we go any further, there are two small points to clarify. The first is, whether "turning into a different person" (v. 6) and God's "giving him another heart" (v. 9) refer to the same event. Most commentators agree that this is the case.[23] The second is the matter of the order. The prediction is for the "turning into a different person," to take place after all three signs have taken place, but verse 9 places the giving of a new heart immediately after this prediction, that is, before the fulfillment of the signs. This caused some commentators to move this phrase after v. 10.[24] However, many take this as part of the summary statement.

The Nature of Saul's Experience with the Spirit

A number of studies point out a close link between the first monarch and the prophetic movement. In this chapter, we find already that Saul was anointed by the prophet, met by the sons of the prophet, experienced

---

[23] For example, P. Kyle McCarter, Jr., *1 Samuel: A New Translation with Introduction, Notes and Commentary*, Anchor Bible 8 (Garden City, NY: Doubleday, 1980), 183.

[24] For example, Hans Wilhelm Hertzberg, *I & II Samuel*, trans. J. S. Bowden, Old Testament Library (Philadelphia: Westminster, 1964), 77.

the prophetic Spirit, and even linked with the prophetic guild by a popular saying. But more importantly, the entire "Former Prophets," to which this book belongs, present and evaluate the national history of Israel according to prophetic standards. The prophetic tradition stands "as a refreshing counterpoise to the potential despotism of the monarchy."[25]

The third sign involved Saul's journey to Gibeath-elohim (1 Sam 10:5), where he encountered the "sons of the prophet," coming down from a high (cultic) place, "prophesying," presumably under the influence of the Spirit and accompanied by music. Then the Spirit of God rushed upon him, and he also began to prophesy along with the prophetic guild. The hithpael form of the verb נבא is generally understood as referring to prophetic trance or ecstatic behavior.[26] The presence of music and the absence of any oracular activity also support this interpretation.

Throughout the Old Testament, there are several references to "a new heart" or "a different heart." As "heart" and "spirit" are often used in the Hebrew Bible either interchangeably or parallel with each other, "a new spirit" may be considered in this survey. The psalmist pleads for God to "create . . . a clean heart . . . and put a new and right spirit" within him (Psa 51:10). In three places, Ezekiel declares God's promise for forgiveness and a radical transformation using the same terms. "A new heart I will give you, and a new spirit I will put within you" (Ezek 36:26). In a parallel passage, a different expression is used: "I will remove the heart of stone from their flesh and give them a heart of flesh" (Ezek 11:19). The prophet admonishes Israel, "Cast away from you all the transgressions that you have committed against me, and get yourselves a new heart and a new spirit!" (Ezek 18:31). "A new or different heart" (or

---

[25]Ronald F. Youngblood, "1, 2 Samuel," *Expositor's Bible Commentary* 3 (Grand Rapids, MI: Zondervan, 1992), 624.

[26]The distinction between the two common verbal forms (the other being the niphal form) is not straightforward. See a useful discussion in Robert R. Wilson, *Prophecy and Society in Ancient Israel* (Philadelphia: Fortress, 1980), 137–38.

"a new spirit") is an exclusive expression for a radical inner transformation to return to God and align to his will. The result of the "new heart" in Ezek 11 is telling: ". . . so that they may follow my statutes and keep my ordinances and obey them" (Ezek 11:20). This radical transformation is all attributed to a divine action, far beyond human behavioral change.

Then in Saul's case, to what does this radical transformation, that is turning to "a different person" or having "a new heart," specifically refer? A number of scholars believe that this refers to the prophetic experience he was to have among the sons of the prophet. For example, in an extremely useful book on the three first kings of Israel, T. Czövek, frequently using Polzin for this passage, argues that there was a sort of prophetic conspiracy to restrict this new kingship under the firm prophetic control.[27] Although a close examination of this point is reserved below, it is less convincing for the following reasons. First, Saul's prophetic experience was temporal, and he was not intended to remain in the company of the prophets. The riddle which was later associated with him ("Is Saul among the prophets?") begs a response, "Of course not." Second, the unusual endorsement recorded in v. 7 (then ". . . do whatever you see fit to do, for God is with you") does not naturally fit the prophetic experience. It may be better suited to a military undertaking. Third, as briefly observed above, the "new heart" throughout the Old Testament points to an inner transformation rather than anything external. And, fourth, the nature of this promise refers to Saul's discretionary action, which is quite different from the invasive and overwhelming (and sometimes demobilizing) nature of the prophetic experience.

---

[27]Tamás Czövek, *Three Seasons of Charismatic Leadership: A Literary-Critical and Theological Interpretation of the Narrative of Saul, David and Solomon* (Oxford: Regnum Books, 2006), 57–58.

Then Saul's experience is "a radical transformation of personality," as Parker rightly argues,[28] that is, an inner transformation. Such a divine blanket endorsement is possible only when a human heart is in a complete alignment with God's will. This also presupposes God's complete approval and his enduring presence. In the spirit of a great degree of ambiguity in the text and also perplexity in Saul's mind, this is a reasonable conclusion we can safely make.

The Role of the Spirit Experience

Then what is this radical transformation for? As introduced above, there has been a strong argument that there was a political motivation to maintain a prophetic control over kingship. Like many others, Czövek acknowledges the ambiguity of the passage both to the readers and to Saul. However, he maintains that the intention of the narrator is increasingly clear: "[he has become] a dupe at the prophet's disposal, created with God's assistance, as 10:9 suggests."[29] Through this process, Saul is no longer "the son of Kish and in his father's service; from now on he will be the son of Samuel."[30] Saul's experience was to demonstrate "how impressive a prophetic power can be."[31] Accordingly, Czövek rephrases v. 7 to mean, "If you listen to me, you will do whatever you like to."[32] Only when Saul was to become both king and prophet, a "double warrant for royal dependence on Samuel" is achieved, thus, achieving the prophet's control over the king.[33] This religious experience, according to

---

[28]Simon B. Parker, "Possession Trance and Prophecy in Pre-Exilic Israel," *Vetus Testamentum* 28:3 (1978), 272.

[29]Czövek, *Three Seasons*, 57.

[30]Nico ter Linden, *The Stories of Judges and Kings*, The Story Goes, 3, trans. John Bowden (London: SCM, 2000), 95.

[31]R. Polzin, *Samuel and Deuteronomist: A Literary Study of the Deuteronomistic History, Part 2: 1 Samuel* (Bloomington and Indianapolis, IN: Indiana University Press, 1989), 105.

[32]Czövek, *Three Seasons*, 58.

[33]Polzin, *Samuel and Deuteronomist*, 106; also Czövek, *Three Seasons*, 59.

this interpretation, was a political means to set a paradigm of hegemony for prophetism over kingship.

This perspective puts a strong emphasis on the power dynamic in the formative stage of Israelite kingship. In fact, Samuel viewed the demand for kingship as the people's rejection of theodicy or the political authority of Samuel. However, for the reasons I presented above, it is unlikely that the entire experience, including his experience with God's Spirit, was to keep Saul in the company of the prophets, over which Samuel exercised a decisive control. It is important to be reminded that this is part of the call narrative, and the "rushing" of the Spirit upon Saul is the most critical part of the call process. During the wilderness era, Israel witnessed the link between the "call," the Spirit, and "prophesying." Numbers 11 records Moses' election of seventy elders as his administrative assistants. God authenticated his selection of them by granting the Spirit to them: "[God] took some of the Spirit that was on him and put it on the seventy elders; and when the spirit rested upon them, they prophesied. But they did not do so again" (Num 1:25). In this "call" account, the "prophesying" served as a sign of the presence of God's Spirit, which in turn served as a sign of God's election:

> [P]rophesying was perhaps one of the best phenomena which includes objectivity, demonstrability as well as its cultural acceptability among the Israelites. This visible demonstration of the Spirit's presence was probably intended to provide an objective sign of God's authentication upon the seventy elders to the people.[34]

In this case, the link between the prophesying and the presence of the Spirit is clear: the former serves as a sign of the latter. In fact, this link is more prevalent within the prophetic tradition. It is hard to suspect, therefore, any political agenda in arranging a prophetic experience, if it

---

[34]Wonsuk Ma, "'If It Is a Sign: An Old Testament Reflection on the Initial Evidence Discussion," *Asian Journal of Pentecostal Studies* 2:2 (1999), 163-75, 167.

is at all possible. I imagine that not everyone who was around the sons of the prophet also prophesied as Saul did.

Parker, on the other hand, hints that Saul experienced the conferral of extraordinary power from God through the Spirit.[35] He may have taken Samuel's command for Saul to journey to "Gibeath-elohim, at the place where the Philistine garrison is" (1 Sam 10:5) as an important clue. However, the passage does not show any military significance of Saul's experience in this place. In fact, the link between the Spirit and military exploit comes in ch. 11. Firth also observes a historical development of the Spirit's role on the charismatic leaders: from the empowerment for deliverance (especially among the judges) to exclusively serving as a sign of God's election to leadership (as in David). According to him, Saul is situated in the middle of this continuum, presumably with a possibility of the Spirit's empowerment for military activities, although less prominent by now.[36] McCarter pays attention to the stereotypical verb used here, "[the Spirit will] rush (צלח) upon [you]." The verb is normally used to refer to a military exploit, but here, instead, it refers to prophetic ecstasy.[37] It is therefore not plausible to place the coming of the Spirit as an empowerment for military purposes. The whole narrative of Saul's call including his experience of the Spirit is dominated by prophetic elements, although he was not to be a prophet.

Then the only possible role for the Spirit's coming upon Saul is to authenticate his election as Israel's king through the anointing by Samuel. As observed in Num 11, a human element was affirmed by God through the coming of his Spirit, sometimes with a resultant prophetic experience. And this tended to be temporary and also a behavioral expression rather than an oracular one. In this passage, Samuel's election of Saul now becomes God's election. This sign was essential to the perplexed Saul, as well as to the apprehensive Samuel. The experience

---

[35]Parker, "Possession Trance," 272.
[36]Firth, "Historical Books," 19. Also Czövek, *Three Seasons*, 57.
[37]McCarter, *1 Samuel*, 183.

must have been striking and radical to Saul, thus serving as a sure sign of God's election (but known only to him and Samuel at this time).

Then, does the Spirit's rushing upon Saul serve only to signify the Spirit's presence externally? The language of the passage adds enough weight to the assumption that a radical inner transformation may also be referred to here. McCarter rightly observes the effect of the Spirit's presence as "a loss of self, or rather, the emergence of a new self."[38] God's blanket endorsement of Saul's subsequent actions (v. 7) is an extremely rare statement throughout the Bible, although some commentators believe it is intended to be an attack on the Philistines.[39] The only comparable ones may mostly refer to the future king or the Servant: e.g., "my servant, whom I uphold, my chosen, in whom my soul delights" (Isa 42:1). In fact, this passage presents stronger evidence than the Judg 13 for the inner transformative work of the Spirit. In Saul's case, as in Samson's, it is also noteworthy that he is naturally a man of exceptional statue and character (1 Sam 10:21-24). With all these elements put together, it is not unreasonable to conclude that the experience with the Spirit, as in Samson, was meant to enhance Saul's personal and character development as a chosen leader of God.

Conclusion

When this study began, it was already suspected that the two passages might not provide sufficient data to draw any reasonable conclusion, and this suspicion proves to be correct. The Samson passage is particularly difficult, for there is only one verse to work with, and the passage abruptly ends the chapter. The Saul passage, on the other hand, presents more information to picture the process of anointing and

---

[38] McCarter, *1 Samuel*, 183.
[39] For example, V. Philips Long, *The Reign and Rejection of King Saul: A Case for Literary and Theological Coherence* (Missoula: Scholars, 1989), 207.

ensuing signs. However, in both cases, several commonalities are observed:

1. Both passages fall into the same category: Leadership Spirit tradition, which is charismatic in nature;[40]
2. Both have multiple references to the Spirit; thus, they are still better cases to use to look into the inner working of the Spirit in leaders;
3. In both cases, the passages mark the initial experience with God's Spirit in private settings;
4. The subsequent experiences with the Spirit involve military activities;
5. Both had inherited favorable dispositions and upbringings.
6. The coming of the Spirit may serve as a sign of God's election for leadership.
7. This function tends not to include the empowering work of the Spirit for specific tasks.
8. On the other hand, there is textual evidence that the coming of the Spirit in these initial encounters may have a role in enhancing their character development through the realization of divine reality and their calls.

Then what lessons do we learn from this study, and how do we gain a sense to be faithful "people of the Spirit"? These failed charismatic lives suggest several important lessons:

1. As discussed above, the Spirit's coming upon the leaders is not just to turn the recipients into a "fighting machine." On the contrary, we can observe God's careful attention to the "formation" of the heroes before, during, and after the giving of his Spirit;

---

[40]For this classification, see Wonsuk Ma, *Until the Spirit Comes: The Spirit of God in the Book of Isaiah* (London: T & T Clark, 1999), 29-31.

2. However, the effect of the Spirit's presence is contingent upon the human response or the lack thereof. The character formation through the Spirit is a joint work between divine and human;
3. Although leaders and prophets are both considered "charismatic" when it comes to the work of the Spirit, it is the leaders who are more susceptible to character and moral failures, which ultimately leads to spiritual (and also national) failure.
4. The seductive nature of political power places the leaders in a more vulnerable position, thus, requiring a higher level of awareness of God and the need for God's intervention to resist this seduction. The experience with his Spirit may be just that.

As we conclude, in spite of our less-than-fruitful efforts to unearth any work of the Spirit in the ethical or character development in the recipients' lives, the strongest argument may come from other cases of the Spirit encounter. The ideal king in Isa 11, the Servant of God in Isa 42, and ultimately the life of Jesus epitomize the highest form of Spirit-empowerment.

THE CHARISMATIC AND NON-CHARISMATIC ROLES OF THE SPIRIT IN ISAIAH 11:1-5

by Lian Sian Mung

I was privileged to study under Dr. Kay Fountain, who taught me Biblical Hebrew and exegesis at Asia Pacific Theological Seminary. Not only did she help me develop as an exegete, but also shared her life with me, modeling how a Spirit-filled educator should live out the text. To her I offer this essay with great respect and homage.

Introduction

In the book of Isaiah, the theme of Yahweh's רוּחַ is featured most prominently in chapter 11, where the term רוּחַ appears four times (v. 2). While the charismatic role of Yahweh's spirit in Isaiah 11 has captured much attention, its non-charismatic role deserves further exploration.[1]

---

[1] Some monographs and articles on the spirit of God in the OT that deal with the role of the spirit of Yahweh in Isaiah 11 are Hilary Marlow, "The Spirit of Yahweh in Isaiah 11:1-9," in *Presence, Power and Promise: The Role of the Spirit of God in the Old Testament* (ed. David G. Firth and Paul D. Wegner; Downers Grove, IL: InterVarsity Press, 2011), 220-32; Lloyd Neve, *The Spirit of God in the Old Testament* (Tokyo: Seibunsha, 1972), 55-56; George T. Montague, *The Holy Spirit: Growth of a Biblical Tradition* (New York: Paulist, 1976), 40-42; Wilf Hildebrandt, *An Old Testament Theology of the Spirit of God* (Peabody, MA: Hendrickson, 1995), 128-30; and Christopher J. H. Wright, *Knowing the Holy Spirit through the Old Testament* (Downers Grove, IL: InterVarsity Press, 2006), 93-100. While aforementioned monographs deal with the spirit of Yahweh in Isaiah 11, they paid their attention to the spirit's role in empowering the new ideal ruler for his judicial task. Whereas Neve appears to be correct in observing the ethical role of Yahweh spirit, he does not fully develop his idea (see Neve, *The Spirit of God in the Old Testament*, 56). Wonsuk Ma's work, *Until the Spirit Comes: The Spirit of God in the Book of Isaiah* (Sheffield, UK: Sheffield Academic,

Thus, by employing syntactic, semantic, and pragmatic analyses, this essay will investigate how Yahweh's spirit in 11:1-5 not only empowers the recipient for Yahweh's given task (charismatic), but also makes him to delight in the fear of Yahweh (non-charismatic).[2] That reverential fear is the essential virtue of a just ruler and the foundation of Israelite wisdom, so that the recipient's attitude, thoughts, and behavior may be fully congruent with Yahweh's intention. In the following, we will examine the role of Yahweh's spirit in Isaiah 11:1-5 within its co-texts.

The Co-Texts of Isaiah 11:1-5

While some commentators have suggested that the immediate context of Isaiah 11:1-5 begins from 10:5,[3] this essay proposes that 11:1-5 belongs to the larger literary context of Isaiah 7-12 because of the thematic and linguistic links that support the coherence of 7-12.[4] First, the theme of trusting in Yahweh rather than in foreign alliances is a prominent one throughout chapters 7-12, which is set in the context of

---

1999), 33-42, has dealt with the role of Yahweh's spirit in Isaiah 11; unfortunately, however, he focuses only on verses 1-2 and concludes that the role of the spirit in this passage is to serve as "a sign for a legitimate leader" and to equip him "for the administration of justice and righteousness (see Ma, *Until the Spirit Comes*, 68). Although he is correct in arguing that the spirit of Yahweh enables the ideal ruler to administer his judicial task (charismatic), he has not fully addressed how the endowment of Yahweh's spirit affects the recipient's relationship with Yahweh (non-charismatic).

[2]In this essay, I adopt Wonsuk Ma's definition of "charismatic" and "non-charismatic" roles/traditions of Yahweh's spirit. Whereas the charismatic role denotes the spirit's role to "equip, enable or empower a selected individual to perform a divinely commissioned task," the non-charismatic role refers to the spirit's function to empower "the immediate recipient without an intended consequence for a secondary group of people." See Ma, *Until the Spirit Comes*, 29, and his essay on "The Charismatic Spirit of God," in *Mission in the Spirit: Towards a Pentecostal/Charismatic Missiology* (Oxford, UK: Regnum Books Int'l, 2010), 29.

[3]See Paul D. Wegner, *An Examination of Kingship and Messianic Expectation in Isaiah 1-35* (New York: Edwin Mellen Press, 1992), 234; and also John Oswalt, *The Book of Isaiah: Chapters 1-39* (New International Commentary on the Old Testament; Grand Rapids, MI: Eerdmans, 1986), 54-64; 192-95.

[4]Scholarly opinions differ on whether verses 6-9 is a later addition and if verse 10 belongs to verses 1-9 in the final form of the text. However, since my main concern is not the growth and formation of the text but rather the final form of the text, determining whether Isaiah 11:6-9 belongs to an exilic or pre-exilic period is beyond the scope of this essay. Because of the limited space, this essay limits its scope to verses 1-5.

the Syro-Ephraimitic crisis (see 7:1-9; 8:11-14, 17; 10:20-27; 12:2).[5] Second, the theme of Assyria is prominent throughout chapters 7-11 (see 7:17, 18, 20; 8:4-7; 10:5, 12, 24, 27-34; 11:11, 16). Third, chapter 12 is linked to chapters 7-10 in terms of the theme of trust in Yahweh (e.g., 12:2 //10:20-27), the theme of Zion (e.g., 12:6 //10:24 cf. 8:18; 10:12; 10; 32), and the concept of fear (e.g., 12:2 // 7:4; 8:12; 10:24; 11:2-3).

These above textual links, therefore, suggest that Isaiah 11:1-5 needs to be examined not only in the context of 10:5-12:6, but also in the context of chapters 7-12, which, in turn, belongs to the larger literary block of Isaiah 1-12. Thus, in the final form of the text, chapter 11 is placed in the literary context of the prophetic oracles, which are concerned not only with the king's/ruler's failure to practice justice for the poor and the weak (e.g., 10:1-4), but also with the attitude and character of the kings/rulers of Judah/Israel in 10:1-4 (cf. 1:23), the arrogant Assyrian king in 10:5-19; 27-34, and the people of Judah/Israel (e.g., 9:13[14]; 10:21-22) toward Yahweh and their relationship with Him. In this context, the prophet envisions the coming of the ideal ruler as a new David in Isaiah 11.

In the following section, we will exegetically investigate the role of Yahweh's spirit in 11:1-5 in the light of the above architecture of the text.

An Analysis of the Prophetic Discourse in Isaiah 11:1-5

A Shoot from the Stump of Jesse: A New David (Isa 11:1)

The prophetic oracle in chapter 11 begins with a *WeQatal* verb וְיָצָא ("and it will come up"), which announces the emergence of a shoot from the stump of Jesse (v. 1). The use of a *WeQatal* signifies that 11:1a is syntactically dependent on the previous verse (i.e., 10:34). The

---

[5]See Richard Schultz, "Isaiah, Book of," in *Dictionary for Theological Interpretation of the Bible* (ed. K. J. Vanhoozer. Grand Rapids, MI: Baker, 2005), 339.

syntactical relationship between 10:34 and 11:1 indicates that the rise of a shoot from the stump of Jesse in 11:1 should be understood in contrast with the fall of the Assyrian King in 10:34.⁶ Whereas 10:34 depicts Yahweh's plan to cut down the lofty trees, which represent the Assyrian king, 11:1 reveals his plan to raise up a new ruler from the stump of Jesse. Although verse 1 does not explicitly state that Yahweh will cause a shoot to come out of the stump of Jesse, the coming of Yahweh's רוּחַ upon the shoot in verse 2 signifies that Yahweh is the one who will raise up a shoot (חטר) from the stump (גזע).⁷

While the name "David" (דָּוִד) is frequently mentioned in Isaiah 1-39,⁸ chapter 11 uses the term "Jesse" (יִשַׁי) to refer to the origin of the new ideal ruler ("a shoot from the stump of Jesse" v. 1; cf. v. 10). In 1 Samuel and 2 Kings, only David and no other king in the Davidic monarch is identified as the "son of Jesse,"⁹ implying that the term יִשַׁי in Isaiah 11:1 not only signifies the humble beginning of a ruler, but also recalls the authentication of David as Yahweh's chosen king of Israel through the anointing and the coming of Yahweh's spirit upon him (1 Sam 16:13).¹⁰ Thus, when 11:1 is read in the light of chapters 7-12, it stands out that a shoot from the stump of Jesse does not refer to Ahaz, who failed to put his trust in Yahweh during the Syro-Ephraimitic invasion (see Isa 7-8) but to a new David, who will serve as Yahweh's faithful agent through the empowerment of Yahweh's רוּחַ (11:2-5). This becomes more evident in verse 2, which depicts the coming of Yahweh's רוּחַ upon a new ideal ruler.

---

⁶See Willem Beuken, "'Lebanon with Its Majesty Shall Fall. A Shoot Shall Come Forth from the Stump of Jesse' (Isa 10:34-11:1): Interfacing the Story of Assyria and the Image of Israel's Future in Isaiah 10:11," in *The New Things: Eschatology in Old Testament Prophecy* (ed. F. Postma, K. Spronk and E. Talstra; Amsterdamse Cahiers voor exegese van de Bijbel en zijn Traditties (Maastricht: Uitgeverij Shaker, 2002), 27.

⁷Beuken, "Lebanon with Its Majesty Shall Fall," 29-30.

⁸See, for instance, בֵּית דָּוִד "the house of David," (Isa 7:2; 22:22); כִּסֵּא דָוִד "the throne of David" (Isa 9:6); בְּאֹהֶל דָּוִד "in the tent of David" (Isa 16:5).

⁹See, for instance, 1 Samuel 16:11, 18; 17:58; 20:31; 2 Samuel 23:1; 1 Kings 12:16.

¹⁰See Ma, *Until the Spirit Comes*, 37; Wegner, *Kingship and Messianic Expectation*, 233; Howard, "The Transfer of Power from Saul to David in 1Sam 16:13-14," 475.

The Coming of Yahweh's רוּחַ Upon a New David (Isaiah 11:2)

The pronominal phrase עליו ("upon him") in verse 2a (עָלָיו רוּחַ יְהוָה וְנָחָה) refers back to a new ideal ruler ("a shoot from the stump of Jesse") in the preceding verse. Since the coming of Yahweh's רוּחַ upon a new Davidic figure in verse 2 recalls the coming of the רוּחַ of Yahweh upon David in 1 Samuel 16:13,[11] exploring the relationship between the two references will help us to better understand the role of Yahweh's רוּחַ in relationship to the new Davidic figure in Isaiah 11:1-5.

The simultaneity of David's anointing with oil and his receipt of Yahweh's רוּחַ in 1 Samuel 16:13 signifies that David was Yahweh's chosen king, "the man after God's own heart/mind" (cf. 1 Sam 13:14).[12] In the context of 1 Samuel 16:13-14, the coming of Yahweh's רוּחַ upon David was followed by its departure from Saul, implying that the רוּחַ of Yahweh that "bestows the gifts necessary for leadership cannot be given to two supreme leaders at the same time."[13] According to Block, the coming of Yahweh's רוּחַ upon David in 1 Samuel 16:10 is "a most significant turning point in the history of Israel and her monarchy—the transfer of divine authority and support from Saul to David."[14] The phrase "from that day forward" (מֵהַיּוֹם הַהוּא וָמָעְלָה) in 1 Samuel 16:13c is particularly significant in this context because it signifies that, unlike the judges and Saul on whom Yahweh's רוּחַ came "several different times, (implying it had left

---

[11] The connection between these two references has been long observed. See, for instance, Brueggemann, *Isaiah 1-39*, 99; Oswalt, *The Book of Isaiah: Chapters 1-39*, 279; Kaiser, *Isaiah 1-12*, 256.

[12] Daniel I. Block, "Empowered by the Spirit of God: The Holy Spirit in the Historiographic Writings of the Old Testament," *Southern Baptist Journal of Theology* 1 (1997): 53. Commentators disagree as to whether the phrase אִישׁ כִּלְבָבוֹ in 1Samuel 13:14 refers to "a man of Yahweh's choice" ("according to one's own choosing") or "a man whose heart is like Yahweh's heart." For further information on this debate, see Benjamin Johnson's discussion in his article "The Heart of YHWH's Chosen One in 1 Samuel," *JBL* 131 (2012): 458.

[13] Neve, *The Spirit of God*, 27. See also Howard, "The Transfer of Power from Saul to David in 1 Sam 16:13-14," 479, 480.

[14] Daniel I. Block, "Empowered by the Spirit of God," 51. See also David Toshio Tsumura, *The First Book of Samuel* (NICOT; Grand Rapids, MI: Eerdmans, 2007), 424.

them in some way in the interim periods"),[15] the coming of Yahweh's רוּחַ upon David was to be permanent.[16]

Concerning the role of the coming of Yahweh's רוּחַ, Hildebrand suggests that it equipped David with "military skills and charisma for his leadership skills," which are evident throughout his reign.[17] In 2 Samuel 8:15, David is depicted as Israel's king who administered justice (מִשְׁפָּט) and righteousness (צְדָקָה) to all his people (לְכָל־עַמּוֹ). In 1 Samuel 16:18, the narrator clarifies that David's success in all his undertaking was due to Yahweh's presence in his life—"And David was prospering [lit. 'acting wisely'] in all his ways for Yahweh was with him (דְּרָכָו מַשְׂכִּיל וַיהוָה עִמּוֹ וַיְהִי דָוִד לְכָל)."[18] In summary, the רוּחַ of Yahweh not only authenticated David as Yahweh's chosen king over Israel, but also continually empowered him to carry out his tasks as the one who administered justice and righteousness in his kingdom (cf. 2 Sam 8:15).

Yahweh's Spirit and David (the son of Jesse) in 1 Samuel 16:13

13a - וַיִּקַּח שְׁמוּאֵל אֶת־קֶרֶן הַשֶּׁמֶן: "Then Samuel took the horn of oil,"

13b - וַיִּמְשַׁח אֹתוֹ בְּקֶרֶב אֶחָיו: "and he anointed him in the midst of his brothers,"

13c - מֵהַיּוֹם הַהוּא וָמָעְלָה וַתִּצְלַח רוּחַ־יְהוָה אֶל־דָּוִד: "and *the spirit of Yahweh* rushed *to David* from that day forward."

13d - וַיָּקָם שְׁמוּאֵל וַיֵּלֶךְ הָרָמָתָה: "Then Samuel rose up and went to Ramah."

---

[15]Howard, "The Transfer of Power from Saul to David in 1 Sam 16:13-14," 475.

[16]Neve, *The Spirit of God in the Old Testament*, 23. See also Block, "Empowered by the Spirit of God," 53.

[17]Hildebrandt, *An Old Testament Theology of the Spirit of God*, 126.

[18]Robert D. Bergen, *1, 2 Samuel* (The New American Commentary; Nashville, TN: Broadman & Holman Publishers, 1996), 181.

Yahweh's Spirit and a New David (a shoot from the stump of Jesse) in Isaiah 11:2

2a - וְנָחָה עָלָיו רוּחַ יְהוָה: "and *the spirit of Yahweh* will rest *upon him*,"

2b - 2א רוּחַ חָכְמָה וּבִינָה (*ellipsis*): "the spirit of wisdom and understanding,"

2c - רוּחַ עֵצָה וּגְבוּרָה (*ellipsis*): "the spirit of counsel and might."

2d - רוּחַ דַּעַת וְיִרְאַת יְהוָה (*ellipsis*): "the spirit of knowledge and the fear of Yahweh."

Just as the narrator in the Book of Samuel views that the רוּחַ of Yahweh played a central role in carrying out Yahweh's plan to establish a just and righteous kingdom through the Davidic dynasty after the failure of King Saul (see 1 Sam 16:13-14; 18:14; 2 Sam 8:15), the prophet in Isaiah 11:1-5 also portrays that Yahweh's רוּחַ is fundamental in executing Yahweh's plan to establish his kingdom of righteousness and peace through a new monarch. When Isaiah 11:1-5 is read in association with 1 Samuel 16:13-14, it stands out that "a shoot from the stump of Jesse" in 11:2 may not refer to a king from the Davidic dynasty, but rather a new David who will be empowered to be Yahweh's agent of righteousness through the work of the רוּחַ of Yahweh. Just as David, the son of Jesse, experienced the coming of Yahweh's רוּחַ that authenticated his kingship and empowered him for his task, Yahweh's רוּחַ will come upon the new David, who is identified as a shoot from the stump of Jesse, to endow him with spiritual gifts (v. 2) so that he will delight in the fear of Yahweh (v. 3a) and be able to administer justice and righteousness (vv. 4-5a).

The Use of Genitive of Effect in Isaiah 11:2b-2d

In the following, we will further explore how Yahweh's רוּחַ will equip the new David with three pairs of spiritual gifts that will prepare and empower him to carry out his task as Yahweh's agent of righteousness (vv. 2b-5b). The fourfold repetition of the noun רוּחַ and the double occurrences of the divine name יהוה in verse 2 imply that it is Yahweh who will raise up a new David and equip him through his רוּחַ with the necessary virtues or qualities to carry out his task as Yahweh's faithful agent of righteousness. In Isaiah 11:2b-c, the poet uses 'a genitive of effect' structure, where the three pairs of spiritual gifts are endowed upon a new David. Waltke and O'Conner point out that "in a genitive of effect, the relationship of C and G is a directly causational one, that is, roughly, C causes G."[19]

2a - וְנָחָה עָלָיו רוּחַ יְהוָה: "and the spirit of Yahweh will rest upon him,"

2b - רוּחַ חָכְמָה וּבִינָה: "the spirit (C) *that causes* (G) wisdom and understanding,"

2c - רוּחַ עֵצָה וּגְבוּרָה: "the spirit (C) *that causes* (G) counsel and might,"

2d - רוּחַ דַּעַת וְיִרְאַת יְהוָה: "the spirit (C) *that causes* (G) knowledge and the fear of Yahweh."

Use of the genitive of effect structure in verse 2b-d signifies that the רוּחַ is the agent that induces or causes all the skills and gifts mentioned in the verse. When seen in relationship with the clause וְנָחָה עָלָיו רוּחַ יְהוָה in verse 2a, it can be deduced that the רוּחַ of Yahweh is the source of all

---

[19]Waltke and O'Connor, *An Introduction to Biblical Hebrew Syntax*, § 9.5.2c, 146. See also J. C. L. Gibson, *Davidson's Introductory Hebrew Grammar Syntax* (Scotland: T&T Clark, 1994), § 34, 31.

the three pairs of spiritual attributes given to the new David (vv. 1- 2) for fulfilling his tasks (vv. 3-5).

The first pair—"the spirit (רוּחַ) of wisdom (חָכְמָה) and understanding (בִּינָה)"—is bestowed on the new David for his judicial office so that he would be able to judge (שׁפט) the poor with righteousness (צֶדֶק).[20] In contrast to the Assyrian King who proudly claims that he was able to defeat many nations due to his own wisdom (חָכְמָה) and understanding (בִּין Isa 10:13), the wisdom (חָכְמָה) and understanding (בִּינָה) of the new David are attributed to the רוּחַ of Yahweh, signifying his dependence upon Yahweh.[21]

In 1 Kings 3:12, Yahweh gave a wise (חכמה) and discerning (בין) heart to Solomon (the successor of David) so that he would be able to judge (לִשְׁפֹּט) Yahweh's people and to distinguish between right and wrong (1 Kgs 3:9).[22] Just as Yahweh gave such a heart to Solomon for his judicial office as the king of Israel, the רוּחַ of Yahweh will endow the new David with the רוּחַ of wisdom and understanding to establish a kingdom of justice and righteousness (cf. Isa 11:3-5).

The new David will also be equipped with the second pair of attributes (v. 2c)—"the spirit of counsel and might (רוּחַ עֵצָה וּגְבוּרָה)." In Isaiah 36:5, the noun עצה denotes a 'strategy' or 'plan,' and גְּבוּרָה refers to the 'military strength' to rebel against the Assyrians; thus the phrase "counsel and might (עֵצָה וּגְבוּרָה)" has a military connotation.[23] In this light, it can be suggested that the second pair of the spiritual attributes will enable the new ideal ruler to "plan and act with confidence and

---

[20]See Uppsala Tengström, "רוּחַ rûah," in *Theological Dictionary of the Old Testament* (vol. 13, ed. Johannes Botterweck, Helmer Ringgren, and Heinz-Josef Fabry; trans., David E. Green; Grand Rapids, MI: Eerdmans, 2004), 390-91.

[21]Archibald L. H. M. van Wieringen, *The Implied Reader in Isaiah 6-12* (Leiden: Brill, 1998), 202.

[22]Brevard Childs, *Isaiah* (Old Testament Library; Louisville, KY: Westminster John Knox Press, 2001), 103.

[23]Gary Smith, *Isaiah 1-39* (New American Commentary; Nashville, TN: Broadman & Holman, 2007) 598.

strength, ensuring victory over enemies and adversaries."²⁴ The Israelite wisdom tradition acknowledges that counsel and might/strength belong to God: "With God are wisdom (חכמה) and might (גבורה); he has counsel (עצה) and understanding (תבונה)" (Job 12:13).²⁵ In the same vein, in Proverbs 8:14-16, counsel (עצה), might (גְּבוּרָה 11:2c), and understanding (בִּינָה 11:2b) are depicted as virtues that Lady Wisdom possesses (Prov 8:14), and they are closely associated with kingship and righteous governance.²⁶

8:14a - לִי־עֵצָה וְתוּשִׁיָּה: "Mine are *counsel* (עצה) and sound wisdom (תושיה)."

8:14b - אֲנִי בִינָה לִי גְבוּרָה: "I am understanding (בינה). I have *might* (גבורה)."

8:15a - בִּי מְלָכִים יִמְלֹכוּ: "By me kings reign (מלך)"

8:15b - וְרוֹזְנִים יְחֹקְקוּ צֶדֶק "and rulers decree what is just צֶדֶק"

8:16a - בִּי שָׂרִים יָשֹׂרוּ: "By me princes rule (שׂרר)"

8:16b - וּנְדִיבִים כָּל־שֹׁפְטֵי צֶדֶק: "and nobles, all who govern (שפט) rightly (צֶדֶק)."

The linguistic and thematic connections between the aforementioned texts indicate that the concept of the second pair of the spiritual attributes (רוּחַ עֵצָה וּגְבוּרָה) given to the new David in Isaiah 11:1 recalls the characteristics of an ideal king depicted in the Israelite wisdom tradition. Seen in this light, the purpose of Yahweh's spirit's endowment of the new Davidic ruler in 11:1-5 is to enable him to establish a kingdom of righteousness as Yahweh's agent by ruling (שפט) justly (צֶדֶק) with wisdom and might (vv. 2-4; cf. Prov 8:14-16).

---

[24]Marlow, "The Spirit of Yahweh in Isaiah 11:1-9," 226.
[25]Roland Murphy, *Proverbs* (Word Biblical Commentary; Columbia: Nelson Reference & Electronic, 1998), 51.
[26]See Richard J. Clifford, *Proverbs: A Commentary* (Old Testament Library; Louisville, KY: Westminster John Knox Press, 1999), 95; R. N. Whybray, *Proverbs* (New Century Bible Commentary; Grand Rapids, MI: Eerdmans, 1994), 125.

The third pair—"the spirit of knowledge and the fear of Yahweh (רוּחַ דַּעַת וְיִרְאַת יְהוָה)"—expresses the new ideal ruler's relationship with Yahweh.[27] In Proverbs 1:7, the fear of Yahweh (יִרְאַת יְהוָה) is described as the beginning of knowledge (דַּעַת); and in Proverbs 2:5, the fear of Yahweh (יִרְאַת יְהוָה) is paired with the knowledge of God (דַּעַת אֱלֹהִים).[28] In Isaiah 33:5-6, wisdom (חָכְמָה), knowledge (דַּעַת), and the fear of Yahweh (יִרְאַת יְהוָה) are associated with the establishment of Yahweh's kingdom of righteousness in Zion.[29] In light of our observations above, it may be suggested that the purpose of the endowment of the third pair of spiritual attributes (11:2d) is to make the new David's thoughts and actions "fully congruent and resonant" with Yahweh's will and intention,[30] so that he may serve as Yahweh's faithful agent of righteousness (vv. 3-5). The theme of the fear of Yahweh is further developed in the following verse (v. 3a).

The Roles of Yahweh's רוּחַ in Isaiah 11:3-5

The Non-Charismatic Role of the רוּחַ of Yahweh in Isaiah 11:3a

Commentators are puzzled by the colon in 11:3a וַהֲרִיחוֹ בְּיִרְאַת יְהוָה ("And his delight shall be in the fear of Yahweh").[31] The editors of the *BHS* and some commentators proposed that the colon וַהֲרִיחוֹ בְּיִרְאַת יְהוָה in verse 3a should be deleted because it is textual dittography.

---

[27]Tengström, "רוּחַ *rûah*," in *TDOT* 13: 394. See also Edward Young, *The Book of Isaiah: The English Text, with Introduction, Exposition, and Notes* (vol. 1; Grand Rapids, MI: Eerdmans, 1965), 382.

[28]Kaiser, *Isaiah 1-12* (The Old Testament Library; 2nd ed.; trans. John Bowden; Philadelphia: Westminster Press, 1983), 256.

[29]In his article, Beuken observes how Isaiah 33:5-6 shares the same vocabulary with Isaiah 11:1-9. See "Jesaja 33 als Spiegeltext im Jesajabuch," *Ephemerides theologicae lovanienses* 67 (1991): 16.

[30]Brueggemann, *Isaiah 1-39* (Westminster Bible Companion; Louisville, Ky.: Westminster John Knox Press, 1998), 18.

[31]See Arie Shifman, "'A Scent' of the Spirit: Exegesis of an Enigmatic Verse (Isaiah 11:3)," *JBL* 2 (2012): 249.

Wildberger also argues that "There is no doubt that it is actually a dittography from the previous רוח (דעת) ויראת יהוה spirit of knowledge and of fear of Yahweh" and that "the repetition of יראת יהוה ('fear of Yahweh') interrupts the flow."³² In the same vein, Clements also suggests the clause "should be omitted as a variant reading of the last part of v. 2 which has come into the text."³³ Contrary to the aforementioned views, Motyer sees verse 3a as "a domino link between verses 2 and 3a."³⁴ Thus, the different scholarly opinions on the placement and function of verse 3a in its present literary position reveal a need for a more thorough analysis within its larger context in the book of Isaiah and also in its canonical context.

We begin our investigation by exploring the relationship between the concept of the fear of Yahweh and kingship in Israel in Deuteronomy 17:18-20. In this context, the fear of Yahweh (lit. "to fear Yahweh" (יְהוָה־ אֶת לְיִרְאָה) is described as the essential virtue that an Israelite king is required to possess. In vv. 18-20, the king is required to learn to fear Yahweh through his copying, keeping, writing, and reading of the book of the law הַתּוֹרָה and to demonstrate his fear of Yahweh by keeping (שׁמר) all the words of the law (הַתּוֹרָה) and the statutes (הַחֻקִּים) and doing (עשׂה) them (v. 19). As Craigie observes, since the king's responsibility is to rule on earth on behalf of Yahweh, he has to "do so in line with the holiness and righteousness of Yahweh" (Deut 17:18-19).³⁵ Verse 20 further states that possessing the virtue of the fear of Yahweh keeps the king from

---

³²See Wildberger, *Isaiah 1-12: A Commentary* (Trans. Thomas H. Trapp: Minneapolis: Fortress, 1991), 461.

³³Clements, *Isaiah 1-39* (New Century Bible Commentary; Grand Rapids, Mich.: Eerdmans, 1980)123.

³⁴Motyer, *The Prophecy of Isaiah: An Introduction & Commentary* (Downers Grove, Ill.: InterVarsity, 1993), 123.

³⁵ See Peter Craigie, *The Book of Deuteronomy* (NICOT; Grand Rapids, Mich.: Eerdmans, 1976), 266.

becoming prideful (v. 20a) and turning aside from Yahweh's commandments so that he and his descendants may reign for a long period of time.

In line with the teaching of Deuteronomy 17:18-20 on kingship and the fear of Yahweh, the Israelite wisdom tradition also defines the fear of Yahweh as the beginning of wisdom (Prov 1:7; 9:10) and the hatred of evil, pride, arrogance, evil ways, and a perverse mouth (Prov 8:13). In Proverbs 8:13-16, the fear of Yahweh (v. 13; cf. Isa 11:2d-3a) is closely associated with the theme of wisdom, understanding, and might (v. 14; cf. Isa 11:2b-c) and also with the theme of righteous governance (vv. 15-16; cf. Isa 11:3b-5).

Thematic Progression in Proverbs 8:13-16 and Isaiah 11:2d-5

The Fear of Yahweh as the foundation of Israelite wisdom
(Prov 8:13 // Isa 11:2d-3a)
Result 1: counsel and wisdom, understanding and strength
(Prov 8:14 // Isa 11:2a-c)
Result 2: righteous governance
(Prov 8:15-16 // Isa 11: 3b-5)

In Proverbs 8:13-16, as illustrated above, the fear of Yahweh serves as the foundation of righteous governance (cf. Deut 17:18-20; Isa 11:2-5). Similarly, in David's last words in 2 Samuel 23:2-3, the concept of the fear of God is closely linked with the theme of righteous governance. These words were known as the "oracle of David, the son of Jesse (בֶּן־יִשַׁי), and the anointed (מָשִׁיחַ) of the God of Jacob, who spoke through the רוּחַ of Yahweh (v. 2)."

2a - רוּחַ יְהוָה דִּבֶּר־בִּי: "The *Spirit of Yahweh* speaks through me,"
2b - וּמִלָּתוֹ עַל־לְשׁוֹנִי: "and his word is upon my tongue."
3a - אָמַר אֱלֹהֵי יִשְׂרָאֵל לִי: "The God of Israel said to me,"

3b - לִי דִּבֶּר צוּר יִשְׂרָאֵל: "the Rock of Israel spoke to me,"

3c - מוֹשֵׁל בָּאָדָם צַדִּיק: "the one who *rules* over men *in righteousness*"

3d - מוֹשֵׁל יִרְאַת אֱלֹהִים: "the one who *rules in the fear of God.*"

Thus, the aforementioned texts reveal that the fear of Yahweh is closely associated with righteous governance and also with keeping Yahweh's commandments (Deut 17:18-20), and the hatred of evil and pride (Prov. 18:13; Prov. 1:7; 9:10; cf. Deut 17:20). Just as Deuteronomy 17 describes the fear of Yahweh as the essential virtue that is required for an Israelite king to possess, the oracle of David (2 Sam 23:1-3) and the Israelite wisdom tradition (Prov 8:13-16) also affirm that the fear of Yahweh is indispensable to righteous governance.

While Deuteronomy 17:18-20 teaches that a king has to read the Torah day and night in order to possess the virtue of the fear of Yahweh, Isaiah 11:1-5 envisions that Yahweh's רוּחַ will bestow that virtue on the new David, causing him to delight in the fear of Yahweh so as not become proud (cf. Deut 17:18-20); but rather he will be free from all evil (cf. Prov 8) and will be able not only to keep all of Yahweh's commandments (Deut 17:18-19), but also to govern righteously (2 Sam 23:1-3; Prov 8:15-16).

Seen in the context of Isaiah 7-12, the fear of Yahweh will keep the new David from acting like the arrogant Assyrian king who lifts himself up and speaks boastfully (Isa 10:7, 13-14; cf. Deut 17:20; Prov. 8:13), or Ahaz, the unfaithful Davidic King who failed to put his trust in Yahweh (Isa 7-8), or Judah's contemporary leaders who acted unjustly toward the poor, the fatherless, and the widows (10:1-4; cf. 1:23; 3:14; 5:23).

Therefore, the above observations lead us to deduce that the clause וַהֲרִיחוֹ בְּיִרְאַת יְהוָה in Isaiah 11:3a is not a scribal error which interrupts the flow (contra Wildberger, Clements). In its present literary position, verse 3a functions to ensure that Yahweh's רוּחַ equips the new David to become Yahweh's faithful agent whose thoughts and deeds are fully in harmony with Yahweh's intention to establish his kingdom of righteousness.

In the following verses (11:3b-5), we will further explore how all the spiritual attributes in Isaiah 11:2 equip the new David to carry out Yahweh's plan to establish a righteous kingdom.

The Charismatic Role of Yahweh's רוּחַ: Empowerment for Service (Isaiah 11:3b-4b)

In Isaiah 11:3b, there is a thematic shift from how the empowerment of Yahweh's רוּחַ effects the new David's relationship with Yahweh by empowering him to delight in the fear of Yahweh (v. 3a) to the manner in which he will carry out his task as Yahweh's agent of righteousness (vv. 3b-4). The repetition of the two verbs שפט and יכח in verses 3b and 4b signifies that the two cola in 3b-c are closely linked with the ones in 4a-b.

3b - וְלֹא־לְמַרְאֵה עֵינָיו יִשְׁפּוֹט: "and he will שפט not (לא) by *what he sees*"

3c - וְלֹא־לְמִשְׁמַע אָזְנָיו יוֹכִיחַ: "and he will יכח not (לא) by *what he hears*,"

4a - וְשָׁפַט בְּצֶדֶק דַּלִּים: "but he will שפט *with righteousness*"

4b - וְהוֹכִיחַ בְּמִישׁוֹר לְעַנְוֵי־אָרֶץ: "and he will יכח *with equity*"

While use of the same verbs (שפט and יכח) in both 3b-4b and 4a-b reveals that the two verses are connected, the double use of the negative particle (לא) in 3b-c (לֹא־לְמַרְאֵה: "not by what he sees" and לֹא־לְמִשְׁמַע: "not by what he hears") further clarifies that the two verses are connected in terms of contrast. Whereas verse 3b-c portrays a manner in which he will not carry out his judicial task, the two prepositional phrases (בְּצֶדֶק: "with righteousness" and בְּמִישׁוֹר: "with equity") in verse 4 depict the manner in which he will carry out his task.

Having been equipped with the three pairs of spiritual gifts (v. 2), the new David will not carry out his judicial task like any ordinary kings or judges, who depend on what they can see (לֹא־לְמַרְאֵה) or what they can hear (לֹא־לְמִשְׁמַע). While use of the noun phrases "what he sees" or "what he hears" in Isaiah 11:3b-c may be reminiscent of the theme of a hardening motif in Isaiah 6:10,[36] it is more likely that verse 3b-c recalls 1 Kings 3:28, where Solomon was depicted as having the wisdom of God (חָכְמַת אֱלֹהִים) to administer justice (מִשְׁפָּט).

In the context of 1 Kings 3, the bestowal of a wise (חכ~) and understanding (בִּינָה) heart to Solomon (v. 12) was followed by the narrator's depiction of how Solomon was able to rightly arbitrate a dispute between the two harlots (both of whom claimed to be the mother of the living child) and to bring justice to them. In this case, Solomon's arbitration was not merely based on what the two women said (i.e., what he heard) or the evidence they presented (i.e., what he saw) (cf. 1 Kgs 3:16-28), but he was able to go beyond the evidence presented because Yahweh had given him a heart of wisdom and understanding/discerning (cf. 1 Kgs 3:12). This is affirmed by verse 28, which depicts how the people of Israel were impressed by Solomon's wisdom to judge: "Then all Israel heard the judgment (משפט) that the king had judged (שפט), and they stood in awe (lit. 'fear') before the king because they saw (ראה) that the wisdom of God (חָכְמַת אֱלֹהִים) is in him to administer (עשה) justice (משפט)."

In summary, just as Solomon, who was endowed with a heart of wisdom and discerning, administered justice and righteousness through the wisdom of God that enabled him to go beyond what he could see or hear, the new David's ability to judge and determine the truth will not be limited by what he sees or hears (i.e., the evidence presented to him) because he is equipped with the רוּחַ of wisdom (חָכְמָה) and understanding

---

[36]See Williamson, *Variations on a Theme: King, Messiah and Servant in the Book of Isaiah* (Carlisle, Cumbria: Paternoster, 1998), 49.

The Charismatic and Non-Charismatic Roles of the Spirit in Isaiah 11:1-5

(בִּינָה). It is worth noting, however, that the new David will not be like Solomon, whose heart was turned away to other gods by his foreign wives whom he loved (1 Kgs 11:1-4),[37] or the contemporary rulers of Judah and Jerusalem, who loved bribes and failed to bring justice to the fatherless and widows (10:1-4; 1:23). Yahweh's רוּחַ will empower the new David to delight in the fear of Yahweh (Isa 11:3a) so that he will not fail to keep Yahweh's commandments (cf. Deut 17:18-20). In this way, Isaiah 11:2-3 paves the way for verse 4a-d, which portrays the manner in which the new David will bring justice, righteousness, and order in the society.

In verse 4, the speaker employs a series of word plays (שׁפט: he will judge // שׁבט: rod // שׂפה: lip), which function as a powerful linking to bond the couplet together.[38] Use of these word plays signifies that the role of the spirit-empowered ruler is both to judge (שׁפט) the poor with righteousness (v. 4a-b) and to punish the wicked with the rod (שׁפט) of his mouth and with his lips (שׂפה) (v. 4c-d). The clause וְשָׁפַט בְּצֶדֶק דַּלִּים ("and he will judge the poor") in 4a is "an expression of a royal role not only in Israel but across the ancient Near East."[39] For instance, Hammurabi, in the prologue to his laws, states that the gods Anum and Enlil commissioned him "to cause justice to prevail in the land, to destroy the wicked and the evil, that the strong might not oppress the weak."[40] The same concept concerning the king's responsibility to protect the poor and to crush the wicked (oppressor) is also found in Psalm 72.

Psalm 72 begins with a prayer for the king to be endowed with God's justice (lit. "your justice" מִשְׁפָּטֶיךָ) and his righteousness (lit. "your

---

[37]Lissa M. Wray Beal, *1 & 2 Kings* (Apollos Old Testament Commentary; Downers Grove, IL: InterVarsity Press, 2014), 90-91.

[38]Watson, *Classical Hebrew Poetry: A Guide to Its Technique* (London: T & T Clark, 2005), 245.

[39]Oswalt, *Isaiah: Chapters 1-39* (NICOT; Grand Rapids, MI: Eerdmans, 1986), 281.

[40]J. B. Pritchard, *The Ancient Near Eastern Texts Relating to the Old Testament NET* (2nd ed., Princeton, NJ: Princeton University Press, 1955), 164; quoted in Joseph Blenkinsopp, *Isaiah 1-39, The Anchor Bible: A New Translation with Introduction and Commentary* (Anchor Bible Dictionary; New York: Double Day, 2000), 265.

righteousness" וְצִדְקָתְךָ) so that he may be able to judge God's people with righteousness (צדק) and the poor with justice (משפט).[41] The Psalmist's prayer acknowledges that God is the source of justice and righteousness for the king, who will intervene for the needy (דל) and the oppressed (עָנִי) and will deliver them from oppression and violence as Yahweh's faithful agent of righteousness on earth.

When Isaiah 11:4 is read in relationship with Psalm 72, it stands out that the responsibility of the new ideal ruler is to carry out Yahweh's plan to establish a community of righteousness by defending the rights of the oppressed (v. 4a-b) and the poor and also by punishing the wicked (v. 4b-c). Just as God will bestow his justice and righteousness on the king to intervene for the poor (Ps 72:1-4, 12-14), Yahweh's רוּחַ will also endow the three pairs of spiritual attributes to the new David for his task (Isa 11:1-4). While the רוּחַ of wisdom and understanding (v. 2b) will enable him to judge (שפט) the poor with righteousness (צדק) and decide (יכח) with equity for the oppressed of the land (v. 4a-b), the רוּחַ of counsel and might (v. 2c) will also empower him to slay the wicked (v. 4c-d). In Isaiah 25:4, Yahweh is depicted as a refuge (מָעוֹז) to the poor (דל) and to the needy (אביון) amidst the threat of the ruthless (עריץ). When 11:1-4 is read in association with 25:4 and Psalm 72, it is evident that the new David, empowered by the רוּחַ of Yahweh, is Yahweh's agent to intervene for the poor and oppressed by establishing a righteous community.

Characteristics of a Spirit-Filled Ruler (Isa 11:5)

In Isaiah 11:5, the prophet portrays the character of the new David: "And righteousness (צֶדֶק) will be the girdle of his waist, and faithfulness (אמוּנָה) will be the girdle of his loins." The song of Moses in Deuteronomy 34 depicts Yahweh as אֵל אֱמוּנָה ("a God of faithfulness") who is without iniquity, righteous (צדיק), and upright (cf. v. 4). Similarly, in the book of

---

[41]Knut M. Heim, "The Perfect King of Psalm 72: An Intertextual Inquiry," in *The Lord's Anointed* (ed. P. E. Satterthwaite, Richard Hess, Gordon Wenham; Carlisle, UK: Paternoster, 1995), 235.

Psalms, the two terms צדק and אֱמוּנָה, are frequently used in relationship with Yahweh's character and action in the context of Yahweh's judgement of the earth (96:13), of issuing his decrees in righteousness and in faithfulness (119:138), and of the Psalmist's prayer according to Yahweh's faithfulness and righteousness (143:1). In the book of Isaiah, the term אֱמוּנָה is also used to portray Yahweh's faithfulness in accomplishing wonderful deeds in history according to his divine plan (25:4).[42] Isaiah 33:5-6 depicts Yahweh as the stability (אמונה) of the citizens of those who dwell in a transformed Zion that Yahweh will fill with justice (משפט) and righteousness (צדקה).

While the above observations reveal that both of the terms צדק and אֱמוּנָה are used in relationship with Yahweh's character and his action, it is also worth noting that Yahweh requires Israel to be a people of אמונה ("faithfulness," Jer 5:1)[43] and expects צדק ("righteousness") from them (Isa 5:7). Therefore, seen in light of the above observations, Isaiah 11:5 clarifies that Yahweh's רוּחַ will enable the new David to reflect God's righteousness and faithfulness in the way he will carry out his judicial task as Yahweh's faithful agent. In summation, the divine gifts of wisdom, understanding, counsel, and might (Isa 11:2b-c) will enable the new ruler to judge the poor and the oppressed with (צדק) righteousness (11:5; cf. 11:4; Ps 72:1-4, 12-14; Ps 96:13); and the divine gift of the spirit of the fear of Yahweh (11:2d-3c) will also enable him to demonstrate his faithfulness (אמונה) toward Yahweh (v. 5b).

Conclusion and Implications for Pentecostal Pneumatology

In contrast to the unfaithful Davidic king (Isa 7-8), the unjust leaders who failed to practice justice (10:5), and the arrogant Assyrian king whom Yahweh will bring down (10:33; 5-19, 28-33), Isaiah envisions that Yahweh will raise up a new David who will be empowered by Yahweh's

---

[42]See Smith, *Isaiah 1-39*, 429; Childs, *Isaiah*, 184.
[43]See R. W. L. Moberly, "אמן (*'mn*)," *NIDOTTE* 1: 430.

spirit to become Yahweh's faithful agent of righteousness to establish his kingdom of righteousness and peace (11:1-5; cf. 8:23-9:6). Yahweh's spirit in 11:1-5 not only equips the new ideal ruler with spiritual gifts for his judicial task to administer righteousness and justice by intervening for the poor and the weak (*charismatic*), but also makes him to delight in the fear of God (*non-charismatic*), which serves as the ground of the just reign and the essential virtue of a just ruler and the foundation of Israelite wisdom. The fear of Yahweh, which will result from the non-charismatic function of Yahweh's spirit, will keep the new David from failing to keep Yahweh's commandments (cf. Deut 17:18-20).

While the non-charismatic role of Yahweh's spirit makes the new David become Yahweh's faithful agent whose delight is in the fear of Yahweh, the charismatic function of Yahweh's spirit empowers him to carry out Yahweh's given task, which is to establish a kingdom of righteousness. This implies that a new David (the recipient) in Isaiah 11:1-5 can become Yahweh's faithful agent who effectively carries out that task only through his experiences of the coming of Yahweh's spirit that makes him delight in the fear of Yahweh (non-charismatic) and also empowers him to carry out the task (charismatic).

The above finding has implications for Pentecostal pneumatology. Since the beginning of modern Pentecostalism, the doctrine of Spirit-baptism, which is grounded on Luke-Acts, has been one of the major concerns of Pentecostals. They have argued that the coming the Spirit upon the disciples in Acts 2 was to endow with power for witness (cf. Acts 1:8). While Pentecostals are justified in arguing that the charismatic role of the Spirit empowers the recipients to become effective witnesses based on Luke-Acts, our exegetical analysis of Yahweh's spirit in Isaiah 11:1-5 reveals that it is the non-charismatic role of the Spirit that makes the recipient become Yahweh's faithful agent whose thoughts and actions are fully congruent with His intention. This implies, therefore, that in order to become Jesus' faithful witnesses, it is essential for modern

Pentecostals to pay enough attention to both the charismatic and the non-charismatic roles of the Holy Spirit.

WISE PARTICIPATION IN THE DIVINE LIFE: LESSONS FROM THE LIFE OF DANIEL

by Tim Meadowcroft

Introduction

The book of Daniel is about Daniel; that is why it is called the book of Daniel. That may sound like a statement of the obvious, but in fact the book of Daniel is not often read as if it really were about Daniel. More often, it is read as a combination of disembodied life lessons from the court stories and coded predictions of the future from the visions. With respect to the visions, even where there is caution about the visions as predictive for our own day, there is a strong focus on the emergence of the final kingdom with the accompanying message that God is in control. Very few writers look in depth at what is actually going on for Daniel himself as the book unfolds. Yet there is much to learn from doing so.[1] And in the process, there is much to learn about what it means for the believer to say that God is in control.

In this essay, I argue that the experience of Daniel, and occasionally also that of his three friends, has much to say about the wise participation of the people of God in the life of God. I will show that there is continuity of both the literary expression of participation and of wisdom

---

[1] It is a privilege to contribute to this *festschrift* for Kay Fountain. She has spent much of her life concerned to read the Old Testament well in the purpose of forming leaders in the church. For Kay, this included reading the story of Esther, a Jew who sought be faithful within the empire. This article is about another Jew, Daniel, who also sought to be faithful within the empire, and who in the process tells us much about wise leadership.

terminology throughout the book. In light of that, the nature of wise participation is illuminated by a theological consideration of the vision of the throne room scene and the one like a son of man with respect to the saints of the Most High. This line of reasoning is evident in the court tales,[2] but I will argue it in more detail regarding Daniel's experience of the visions. What emerges is a picture of wise participation in the divine life, comprising subtle interactions between temporal and eschatological understandings, and between the availability and hiddenness of the wisdom of God.[3]

Critical Considerations

I do not want to spend too much time discussing technical critical issues in the study of Daniel, of which there are many. But I do need to outline two particular positions that undergird this article. As is well known, Daniel 1 is in Hebrew before the text switches to Aramaic at 2:4 and remains in Aramaic until the end of chapter 7; chapters 8-12 then revert to Hebrew. There is a consensus of scholarship that the vision chapters are probably later than the court tales. The court tales probably emerge in the Persian period, not long after the events which they recount, while the vision material is probably best dated around the time of the crisis concerning the Greek kingdoms and the abomination of desolation in the 160s BC.[4] Whether they are dated then or not, the vision

---

[2] For some the term "tale" implies non-historical. I use the term as a literary category, not in any sense to pass judgment on the historicity of the material. While there is little external evidence to tie Daniel to a known historical figure, from what we know of the period it is entirely plausible that Daniel is a remembered historical figure on the basis of the text of Daniel.

[3] Aspects of this article are distillations of more fully argued positions in Tim Meadowcroft, "'Beltshazzar, Chief of the Magicians' (NRSV Daniel 4:9: Explorations in Identity and Context from the Career of Daniel," *Mission Studies* 33 (2016): 26-48; "'One Like a Son of Man' in the Court of the Foreign King: Daniel 7 as Pointer to Wise Participation in the Divine Life," *Journal of Theological Interpretation* 10 (2016): 245-63; and "Daniel's Visionary Participation in the Divine Life: Dynamics of Participation in Daniel 8-12," *Journal of Theological Interpretation* 11 (2017), 217-38.

[4] See for example John E. Goldingay, *Daniel* (Dallas: Word, 1989), 328-29.

texts themselves direct the reader to relate the visions to that period of the Jewish experience. My reading assumes that the visions have a particular applicability in the life of the people to the Greek crisis of the second century BC.

Since that material is primarily in Hebrew, what does this say about Daniel 1, which, although set in the court with the other court tales, is written in Hebrew while the other court tales are in Aramaic? One possibility is that chapter one is written later as an introduction to the court stories.[5] As if to say, this is how it came to be that Daniel and his friends are at the imperial court and these are the lessons they learned to help them to be wise in those circumstances. Nobody is able to explain why the book of Daniel is written in two different languages, but the concept of Daniel 1 as introduction to the book as a whole is a helpful one. It allows us to read it as setting the wisdom agenda around which the rest of the book may be read. My reading also makes that assumption.

The Wisdom of God and Daniel in the Court Tales

Daniel, and at times his friends, are wise participants in great events at the Babylonian and Persian courts in Daniel 2-6. The wisdom dynamic is set up in Daniel 1. We can see it by looking in particular at 1:4 and 1:17. The men selected, according to the account (1:4), were to be "versed in every branch of wisdom, endowed with knowledge and insight, and competent to serve in the king's palace."[6] Each of the terms used is freighted with significance to a post-exilic Jewish audience familiar with the wisdom tradition. They were "versed in every branch of wisdom" (literally, "those who are insightful in every wisdom" [*maskilim bekol-chokmah*]). The term *chokmah* might be described as the generic term for matters of skill, morality, attitude towards life experience and a

---

[5]See for example Choon-Leong Seow, *Daniel* (Louisville: Westminster John Knox, 2003), 7-8.

[6]Unless indicated otherwise, I am using the NRSV for scriptural quotations.

response of fear and reverence towards God in the multifarious aspects of human existence. Of course, the call to such *chokmah* finds a response of either wisdom or folly. In the case of Daniel and his friends their approach to the call to wisdom, on the evidence of this phrase, was that of the *maskilim*. The *maskilim* are those whose decisions are characterized by the sort of insight into, and understanding of, the great issues of life that makes success more likely. Once again, this is a word that has strong biblical pedigree. With respect to the book of Daniel, it is a recurring participle in the later chapters (11:33, 35; 12:3, 10). It seems likely that *maskilim* refers to a particular group of people who were faithful under the difficult circumstances occasioned by the invasion of "the Beautiful land" by Antioches IV Epiphanes (11:33, 41).[7]

The phrase "endowed with knowledge and insight" (*yod'ei da'at umvinei mada'*) has been somewhat compressed in translation by the NRSV, as a result of which the young men appear more like recipients of wisdom and less like agents of wisdom than is evident in the Hebrew. In fact, they are those who know (*yod'ei*) and those who understand (*umvinei*). And the objects of the participles describe that which is known and understood by the young sages: knowledge (*da'at*) and thought / understanding (*mada'*). Each of those four terms is used regularly within the Hebrew wisdom tradition. They may have had common currency with their Semitic surrounds (and this usage in Daniel suggests that to be the case), but they were also routine ways of speaking about Hebrew wisdom and would have been recognized as such. Together they speak of the range of abilities and qualities that we associate with intellectual achievement and ability under the wider rubric of Jewish wisdom (*chokmah*).

What is interesting is that the same people who show these qualities are those who are "competent to serve in the king's palace" and are to be

---

[7] See the summary of possibilities and proposal by Paul L. Redditt, "Daniel 11 and the Sociohistorical Setting of the Book of Daniel," *Catholic Biblical Quarterly* 60 (1998): 463-74.

"taught the literature and language of the Chaldeans" (1:4). The text thereby recognizes that the wisdom sought by Nebuchadnezzar, that which would entail the formation of a Babylonian worldview and (subsequent) service in the imperial palace, has something in common with Hebrew ways of expressing wisdom. The wisdom of God is unwittingly being deployed by the King of Babylon in the service of his empire.[8] Godly wisdom is thereby something placed in the service of all humanity, whether that wisdom is acknowledged as such or not. And Daniel, Hananiah, Mishael and Azariah qualify this wisdom by placing it in the service of God and not of the empire.

If this perception of Hebrew wisdom is merely hinted at in the early verses of this introductory narrative, it becomes explicit once we get to the outcome of the training period. At the end of their training period the young men display the same sort of wisdom that was anticipated of them in v. 4 (1:17). They are given "knowledge and skill" (*mada' vehaskeil*). Both terms reflect the earlier description, and again, they are both words that are familiar to those accustomed to the Hebrew wisdom tradition. Additionally, Daniel is given "insight" (*heibin*), again a word also appearing in v. 4 as part of a cluster of terms descriptive of Hebrew wisdom. And the object of this wisdom also has a familiar ring to it: "every aspect of literature and wisdom" (*kol-seipher vekhokmah*). This phrase is a kind of portmanteau combination of the evocative dual focus back in v. 4, namely, the portrait of wisdom in Hebrew terms, and yet a wisdom placed at the service of "the Chaldeans." Now we find that wisdom, unmodified by any limiting adjectives, is linked, not to the literature (*seipher*) of the Chaldeans, but simply to "every aspect of literature." What once looked like wisdom deployed in the service of the Chaldeans has become, by means of the grace of God and the young men's faithfulness during the period of their training, the wisdom of God

---

[8]John J. Collins, *Daniel: A Commentary on the Book of Daniel* (Minneapolis: Fortress, 1993), 138.

at work in Babylon. Thus chapter one sets up the wisdom terms in which the participation of Daniel and his young friends in the great events of their day are to be understood: as the wisdom of God both particular to the people of God and embracing all wisdom.

The Wisdom of God and Daniel in the Hebrew Visions

If this dynamic is programmatic for the book of Daniel as a whole, then we should expect to find wisdom language in the accounts of the visions, or at least in the accounts of Daniel's participation in the visions, and that of his people in the visionary experiences.

The generic wisdom term *chokmah* does not appear at all in chapters 8-12. At first glance this is surprising, given the amount of other wisdom language that does appear. However, the narrative of chapter one uses the term in a generic sense; this level of generality simply does not exist in the vision accounts, which are mostly sharply focused onto particular experiences and events in which the wise man is participant, rather than concerned with general statements about wisdom.

Apart from that, though, it turns out that much of the language used to describe the wisdom of the young men at the beginning and end of their court training reappears in the accounts of Daniel's visionary experiences. This is best illustrated by the clusters of wisdom terms in 1:4 and 17.[9] Daniel needs "understanding" (*b'n*, 1:4, 17) for the vision of chapter eight (8:16, 17, 23, and 27). The angelic interpreters offer this *understanding*, although Daniel routinely falls short of appropriating it. Nevertheless, the aspiration was there. Similarly, as one who has learned the wisdom of literature (1:17), Daniel seeks the *understanding* of Jeremiah's prophecy (9:.2), and once again is offered this *understanding* by the interpreters (9:22, 23). We are not told if this *understanding* was actually achieved on this occasion, but 10:1 assures the reader that this

---

[9] I have used italics to emphasize the occurrences of the wisdom terms that are discussed in the rest of this section.

time, in his third vision, Daniel *understands*. Again, it is with the help of heavenly interpreters (10:12, 14). Strangely, though, in the epilogue to the ensuing vision Daniel himself is less certain than the third person narrator, claiming that he does not *understand* (12:8). Once again, assurance of this *understanding* comes from the heavenly figures (12:10).

The one to whom it is given to "know" (*yd'*, 1.4) is also on a quest for *knowledge* in each of the three visions. As he observes the goat and the ram of chapter eight, an interpreter comes to Daniel in order to cause him to *know* (8:19). Daniel is commanded by the interpreter of the seventy weeks to *know* (9:25), and in 10:20 the "one in human form" (10:18) asks Daniel if he *knows* why he has come (10:20).

The young Jewish men also featured skill or competence (*sakal*, 1.4, 17). Later, one of the failures mentioned by Daniel in prayer on the part of his people is a lack of this very *competence* or *insight* (9:13). But that same *insight* is urged upon Daniel by his interpreters (9:22, 25). Later a reward is offered to these *skilled discerning* ones (12:3), and *understanding* is offered to those who are not the wicked (12:10).

The links continue with the competencies that were endowed, or later urged, on the wise young men as outcomes of their wisdom. One of the results of Daniel's training, as expressed in 1:17, was unanticipated by 1:4, and it entailed Daniel having insight into "visions" (*chazon*) and dreams. This became part of the exercise of Daniel's wisdom in the court tales and continues on in the vision accounts. Given that chapters 8-12 are entirely devoted to the revelatory experiences of the wise Daniel, the one who has *visions*, this is not surprising. As part of the introduction to each of the three vision accounts, we are told that Daniel has a *vision* (8:1; 9:21; 10:14, among others).

The recurrence of the term *'amad* (stand) is also relevant. Because it is a stock verb, with a wide semantic range, care is needed. Nevertheless, its occurrence in the visions is in tune with the evidence adduced above. The king was in search of candidates who would be competent and qualified to *stand* (NRSV "serve," 1:4) in the king's palace. There is a sense of taking a place, and by implication, fulfilling a role.[10] There is also just a hint of resistance about the term; it might in certain contexts have the sense present in the English idiom, "to take a stand." In standing in the king's court these wise men undertake a work of significance, a work that both meets resistance and provides resistance. The verb occurs, then, a number of times in the vision narratives, often simply as descriptive of a physical action, but occasionally with this sense of significance. In 8:4 the other beasts are powerless to *stand* against the ram, as the ram subsequently cannot *stand* against the goat (8:7). In chapter eleven the verb occurs regularly to describe the ability, or inability, of one of the warring parties (the kingdoms of the North and the South) to *resist* the other.[11] Later, one of the angelic beings speaks of his own *standing* (11:1) in support of the prince Michael, who himself *stands* as the protector of Daniel's people (12:1). In the meantime, though, during that first vision Daniel does not distinguish himself by *standing* in response; quite the opposite, in fact. Later in the prologue to the final vision, though, Daniel is told to *stand* (10:11) by those attending him. In doing so he confronts the portentous vision that is being explained to him. Daniel promptly collapses with the declaration, literally, that "there is no strength *standing* [emphasis mine] in me" (10:17). Only at the end does he hear the promise that he will *stand* to receive his allotment at the end of days. But the narrative ends there and we do not know how this worked out for Daniel.

In any case, we see that the role of wisdom continues to be crucial throughout the visions of Daniel 8-12, just as it was in the earlier court tales. Before considering the significance of that further, though, we turn to another significant continuity between the tales and the visions.

---

[10]Goldingay, *Daniel*, 5
[11]11:1, 2, 3, 4, 6, 7, 8, 11, 13, 14, 15, 16, 17, 20, 21, 25, 31.

Wise Participation in the Divine Life: Lessons from the Life of Daniel

Daniel and Daniel's People as Participants

That continuity concerns the participation of Daniel in the narrative. At this point, I do not use the term "participation" in any special or theological sense, but simply to indicate the engagement of Daniel with what is going on. With the court tales there is little that needs to be said. Daniel and/or his friends are evidently participants in the stories which concern them and their engagement with the king and his empire. What is not so evident, though, is that Daniel continues to be a participant as we move into the visions. Yet the visions are not merely visions; they are narratives about a man having visions. This ongoing participation contains an important aspect of the message of the book of Daniel. Let us consider how this is so.

Some aspect of Daniel's visionary experience is recounted in the following verses: 8:1-7, 13-20, 26-27; 9:2-23, 25; 10:1-12, 14-20; 12:4-9, and 13. Thus 66 verses out of a total possible of 133 verses, or 50%, entail the participation of Daniel in the visions described. However, within that, we can treat chapter eleven as a special case, in that it is an extended account of one particular vision and by virtue of its focus on a series of identifiable temporal events. Chapter eleven develops its own narrative momentum while the vision context tends to drop away. If the 45 verses of Daniel 11 are excluded from the calculations, then the percentage of the narrative concerned with participation rises to 75%.

Furthermore, as we will consider below in the context of the throne room scene of Daniel 7, the participation of Daniel in these visionary experiences is in some respects undertaken on behalf of the people. Not surprisingly, then, in addition to the participation of the visionary himself, the people of God (variously described) appear as in some sense participant, or at least affected party, in the following twenty-six verses of Daniel 8-12: 8:10-13, 25; 9:24-27; 11:30-35, 41-45; 12:1-3, and 10-12.[12]

---

[12] The verses of editorial framing have not entered into my calculations.

Allowing for the fact that two of these verses overlap with the list above of those concerning Daniel, 90 of the 133 total verses in Daniel 8-12 are about Daniel or Daniel's people, that is, 68% of the total. Thus, the raw data asks us to take seriously the fact of participation in the visions, and so to consider the participatory experience.

It will be noted that I have not accounted at all for the prayer of Daniel in 9:2-19. Without necessarily a form critical implication that the prayer is out of place in the context in which it appears, Daniel's prayer is anomalous in several respects: it is a prayer; it looks back to what has been rather than forward; it entails both Daniel and the people together; and the response of Gabriel assumes a vision although none has been recounted. While such ambiguities of categorization make it difficult to factor in the prayer of Daniel to the statistical analysis above, if anything, it reinforces the participatory nature of these chapters. A prayer is inherently participatory, and this particular prayer focuses strongly on the experience of Daniel and of his people.

Staying with Daniel and his people as participants in these visions, we find some clear links from chapter seven to subsequent visions around the saints of the Most High. Note in particular 8:23-27, which evokes the interpretation of the court room scene in the previous chapter, albeit without exact linguistic correspondence.[13] Just as the people of the holy ones of the Most High will be worn down by the horn of the fourth kingdom that was making war on them (7:25), so will "the king of bold countenance" destroy the people of the holy ones (8:23-24). Just as the horn of the fourth kingdom, or at least its dominion, will be utterly destroyed (7:26), so will the king of bold countenance be broken (8:25). Furthermore, the destruction of this king will be "not by human hands" (8:25), thus evoking the quarried granite that became the destruction of the great statue of Daniel 2 (8:25, cf. 2:34). Again, the vocabulary is not exact, but the allusion to "not by human hands" creates

---

[13]John J. Collins, *The Apocalyptic Vision of the Book of Daniel* (Ann Arbor: Scholars Press, 1977), 132.

a link between the destruction of the statue and that of the "king of bold countenance." Thus, the vision of Daniel 8 links to the vision of Daniel 2 in the court tales. In the process Daniel 7 and 8 are bound together by a common linking with Daniel 2, and by chapter eight's echoing of the fate and destiny of the holy ones of the Most High. In this way, we are encouraged to read what we have seen of the life of the saints in chapter seven into chapter eight and beyond.

At a technical level, the text beyond chapter eight may be expressed in several ways. First, it is expressed in the relationships between Daniel 8 and 9. In an intriguing analysis, André Lacocque proposes that Daniel 8 and 9 are linked together in a structural schema for what he calls the future facing Hebrew chapters of visions (8-12). He begins with comment on the occurrence of the root *sakal*, which is used in 8:25 with respect to the skills (NRSV, "cunning") of the destructive king. In chapter nine, as we have seen, the same root is used three times with a similar, but differently applied, usage (9:13, 22, and 25).[14] It is used negatively in the prayer of Daniel to speak of the people's failure to exercise understanding. Then it is used twice in the introduction to the interpretation of the vision to express the process of inducing understanding in Daniel. Lacocque sees a further link in that the "desolator" on whom a "decreed end is poured out" (9:27) is a further reflection of the destructive king who eventually is "broken, and not by human hands" (8:25).

Additionally, once the link is made between the experience of the saints in the court room scene and the saints who encounter the king of Greece in chapter eight, and the experience of the saints of chapter eight is linked further into the prayer and interpretation of chapter nine, subsequent mentions of the people, enumerated above, most naturally refer back to the same people who are implicated in the throne room vision. These are they on whose behalf Daniel confesses in his prayer

---

[14]André Lacocque, *Daniel in His Time* (Columbia: University of South Carolina Press, 1988), 10.

(9:15, 16), and with whom he associates himself (9:20). From chapter ten onwards the visionary experience is Daniel's, but his people are regularly kept in view as somehow implicated in what Daniel sees and how he reacts. Thus, Daniel hears from his interpreter (presumably angelic) that the vision of chapter eleven is about "what is to happen to your people" (10:14). Then Daniel is reminded of his people's implication in the great events alluded to by chapter eleven (11:14, 32 and 33), with the tantalising glimpse of dissension and failure amongst those people. Finally, as the vision comes to an end, the angel promises that Daniel's people would eventually and finally be delivered (12:1). In the epilogue that follows, Daniel asks how long all this is to be and receives the enigmatic reply relating to the "holy people" (12:7). Thus, this final mention of Daniel's people evokes the initial description of them as the people of the holy ones of the Most High back in 7:27, who themselves appear in the vision of chapter eight.[15]

With respect to the participation of the people of God in the visions, it has become evident that Daniel is thoroughly immersed within the visions which he has also been observing.[16] As a consequence, the temporal context of Daniel—and hence of his people—is intertwined with that which he is observing. This is experienced acutely in Daniel's person.

Participation in the Divine Life

Having established the continuities in wisdom and participation across the book of Daniel, now let us turn to the question regarding the nature of this participation. Previously we have drawn on the

---

[15]In making this case, I am accepting the view of many commentators that there is an equivalence of some sort between the holy ones of the Most High and the people themselves. See Louis F. Hartman and Alexander A. Di Lella, *The Book of Daniel* (New York: Doubleday, 1978), 100-102.

[16]The related discussion on the interaction of observation and participation as constitutive of the wisdom enterprise, implicit in the title of Paul S. Fiddes, *Seeing the World and Knowing God: Hebrew Wisdom and Christian Doctrine in a Late-Modern Context* (Oxford: Oxford University Press, 2013), is beyond the scope of this article.

significance of Daniel 1 as programmatic for the wisdom dynamic at play through the book. Now we consider the role of Daniel 7 as potentially programmatic for understanding the nature of Daniel's participation in the narrative. It is uncontroversial that Daniel 7 has been regarded as the *literary* hinge on which the book of Daniel swings, concluding as it does the Aramaic court tales and anticipating as it does the visions ascribed to Daniel. I suggest that Daniel 7 may also be read as the *theological* hinge in the book of Daniel:[17] that what we discover theologically arising from the throne room vision and its interpretation is the clue to a fuller appreciation of the theological significance of the wise participation that straddles it.

Thus, we see that the multivalence of the throne room vision of Daniel permits the possibility—invites the possibility, even—of some sort of identification between the one like a son of man and the holy ones of the Most High. At the same time, the one like a son of man and the holy ones of the Most High remain differentiated from each other. Nevertheless, the identification is so close while the differentiation is preserved, that it is possible to describe it in terms of participation. The holy ones of the Most High participate in that into which the one like a son of man has entered as he comes before the Ancient of Days; the people of God participate in the life of God as encountered in that throne room scene. In short, a dynamic occurs that is arguably reflected by the second epistle of Peter's later insight that the faithful "may become participants of the divine nature" made possible through Jesus Christ (2 Pet 1:5).

Much more could be said about this from a Christian and New Testament perspective. However, it is sufficient to say that this dynamic of participation in the divine life hinted at by the throne room vision in

---

[17]See the argument of George Sumner, "Daniel," in Samuel Wells and George Sumner, *Esther & Daniel* (Grand Rapids: Brazos, 2013), 111-14, for Daniel 7 as "the interpretive centre of the book," and in particular his comment: "The thematic center (and almost the actual center of the text) of Daniel is the coming of the 'one like a Son of Man' to the Ancient of Days in Dan. 7."

Daniel 7 has been explored by means of the significance of the incarnation, of the life and significance of the one who himself points to a fulfilment of the vision of one like a son of man.[18] The dynamic of the incarnation is much richer than that God has become one with humanity, and in the process been caught up with all that it means to be human. It turns out that humanity, too, is caught up into the very life of God. To reprise 2 Pet 1:4, humanity participates in the divine life. Others who have expressed the implications of this include T.F. Torrance, who speaks of the "deification" of humanity as the obverse of God's "inhominization" in Christ.[19]

At the same time, this participation in God who has become one with us in Christ has an ethical outcome. As Myk Habets has expressed it, in this intermingling of God and humanity "Christ occupies the central stage in a Christian ethic; ethics is the life of Christ lived out in those savingly united to him."[20] Or, less technically, our participation in the divine nature begs of us the question: how then shall we live? And the answer comes: as those who are caught up with Christ into the very life of God.

Transposing this back to the throne room vision in the book of Daniel, which foreshadows a developed theology of participation in the divine life; those to whom that vision was addressed were called to live wisely as those amongst the people of God who were caught up with the son of man into the very throne room of God. Such wisdom works itself out in the court tales and in the participation of Daniel in the visions that were sent to him.

---

[18]For a full exposition of this position, see Tim Meadowcroft, "'One Like a Son of Man' in the Court of the Foreign King."

[19]T.F. Torrance, *The Trinitarian Faith: The Evangelical Theology of the Ancient Catholic Church* (Edinburgh: T. & T. Clark, 1995), 189, cited in Myk Habets, "'Reformed Theosis?' A Response to Gannon Murphy," *Theology Today* 65 (2009): 491-92.

[20]Myk Habets, "'In Him We Live and Move and Have Our Being': A Theotic Account of Ethics," in ed. Myk Habets, *Third Article Theology: A Pneumatological Dogmatics* (Minneapolis: Fortress, 2016), 417.

The Visionary Participant

We have looked at some of the literary and theological continuities that bind the tales and the visions together. However, if the nature of participation in the divine life that emerges in the book of Daniel is to be appreciated adequately, the discontinuities are also important. For there are some key differences between Daniel's participation in the divine life by means of these visionary encounters, and his participation in the divine life as expressed in his courtly conduct.

At court, Daniel's participation was revelatory to the participant, the intentions of God were evident and reasonable, the resulting wise (and hence ethical) actions achieved a resolution, and the inner life of Daniel (to the extent that it was implied) was characterised by a serene confidence. The one exception to that last comment could be Daniel's initial response to Nebuchadnezzar's dream of the great tree (4:19). Despite the cryptic response to Daniel's terror, he continues on to respond assertively to what he has been shown, culminating in some direct counsel for his employer (4:27). The picture that emerges is of a man confident in his relationship with the king whom he served, and with the God on whose behalf he served.

In the visions, Daniel's participation in the divine life enables him to see much but apparently to understand little; the intentions of God are obscure; there is no temporal resolution and the ethical issues relate less to faithfulness within and with respect to a hostile Gentile environment and more to faithfulness in the struggle for control of the life of the people of God. Further, the inner life of Daniel that emerges is characterised by uncertainty and fragility. In sum, we might say that instead of the certainty of contextually specific divine guidance, there is less certainty and a shift of focus towards the future. The locus of hope is now different. Where hope was once focused onto the behavior of the king, it now shifts towards a more uncertain but more all-embracing eschatological perspective. To put it another way, it entails a commitment to that which cannot always be comprehended or predicted. This too is part of what it means to be amongst the saints of the Most High drawn alongside the throne of the Ancient of Days with the one like a son of man.

The Paradox of Wise Participation

Thus, we see a shift of emphases in the visions with respect to the court tales: a change from present to future, from success to uncertainty, from temporal location to future possibility, from confidence to fear and from history to eschatology with an accompanying allusion to the resurrection (12:3). We also see the shift in ethical focus from wise action to faithful living. At the same time, a quest to see how the discontinuities might talk to each other is validated and encouraged by the continuities we have seen: wisdom terminology, continuity of participation, and a focus on the people of God. One way to discuss the continuity of divine participation across the discontinuities is by means of a paradox.

The paradox occurs around the notion of the hiddenness, or otherwise, of the wisdom of God. In the court tales the results of the young men's wise participation in the divine life are evident and certain. Key ethical decisions are made at key moments and the outcome is decisive in some way. The will of God prevails, lives are preserved, or in some cases judged and destroyed. The king recognizes, albeit usually in his own terms, the activity and reasonableness of "the holy gods" (4:18; 5:11). The hand of God is evident and assumed throughout. From alongside the throne of the Ancient of Days the saints, represented by Daniel and his friends, have exercised the dominion given to them by the fact of their participation. This clarity is refreshing and encouraging, as it has been for many who have read the book of Daniel through the centuries. But it is mysterious to those who read it also, for the clarity and experience of dominion is in the context of an incomplete process. The end is not yet; there is always the potential for another crisis. And, from the perspective of readers, the lived experience of faith is seldom that clear cut. Yet the possibilities within history and the call to ethical responses to life's various contexts are crystal clear.

In the Hebrew visions, although there is considerable continuity, the paradox reverses. Things take a turn to the eschatological; in the light of the present situation, a final resolution is sought and offered. And yet the question of behavior recedes into the background. Instead of to wise action, participation in the divine life now leads to wise affiliation, to loyalty and to faithfulness. But the certain outcome offered by the eschatological vision does not lead to clarity or certainty on the part of the participant. There is no visible resolution.[21] Instead there is uncertainty, and lack of direct access to understanding. The more certain the visions become of the final rule of God, a rule into which the saints themselves are invited to participate, the harder it becomes for the participant to function. At the same time, the more certain the vision the more that suffering begins to impinge on the participant in the divine life.[22] At the point where the reader expects to find relief from the complexities of historical context and the pain of suffering, and to begin to find a final certainty and resolution, uncertainty increases, suffering continues and the hidden or sealed nature of the resolution becomes more explicitly so (12:9).

Whatever else may be intended by the inflation of the time between the "regular burnt offering [being] taken away and the abomination that

---

[21] Danna Nolan Fewell, *Circle of Sovereignty: Plotting Politics in the Book of Daniel* (Nashville: Abingdon, 1991), 135: "The ultimate irony in the book of Daniel, then, is that the kingdom as Daniel envisions it – whether mediated or otherwise – never manifests itself." Fewell describes the "irony" well, but misses the aspect of participation in her attribution of the vision of the kingdom to Daniel. The point is that Daniel is never quite able to envision that which remains hidden.

[22] Although the themes of this article have not been considered explicitly in missiological terms, see with respect to suffering and participation in the mission of God and hence in the life of God, Scott W. Sunquist, *Understanding Christian Mission: Participation in Suffering and Glory* (Grand Rapids: Baker Academic, 2013), 18: "Christian missionary involvement must not be bound to what is popular, popularly known, or even what seems like 'viable' mission. All of the suffering world is the concern of the *missio Dei*, and therefore of our missiology."

desolates [being] set up" in 12:11-12, it compounds the effects noted above. It offers no certainty for the future, and implies that just when a resolution is in sight, the period of uncertainty may be stretched further. This is a regular facet of human experience, inescapable despite the human yearning for certainty. That is perhaps why so many readings of this material in every age have been determined to bring this final hope and define it in terms of contemporary dates and events. But such certainty is simply not available.[23] The more the end is glimpsed the more hidden that end becomes. Thus, the paradox of participation encountered in the court tales is turned on its head by the visionary experience of participation.

This is the hinge around which the participation of the saints in the life of God swings in the book of Daniel.[24] As the saints, we are not God; and God to some extent is hidden from us, and the wisdom of God is correspondingly not fully in view. There is suffering and uncertainty and anguish. The call in the face of an uncertain future is to loyalty and faithfulness to the one who has promised the resolution of history, just as the "end" of the king of the south foreshadows "the end" (11:39-45).[25] At the same time the court tales remind us that, even in the midst of uncertainty, there is a clarion call to wise ethical decision making for action and identification, drawing on the fact that the wisdom of God is available to humanity even where the end may not be fully known. And

---

[23]Paul S. Fiddes, *Participating in God: A Pastoral Doctrine of the Trinity* (London: Darton, Longman and Todd, 2000), 141-42, exploring this in slightly different terms ("an openness about the nature of the world"), comments that "God leaves things open, making space for our contribution to the creative project. This is surely why the predominant note of the Old Testament Scriptures is that of Yahweh's promises for the future, rather than exact predictions."

[24]Goldingay, *Daniel*, 333, notes that this paradox, what he calls "two different overall thrusts," manifests itself "by [the book of Daniel] being located by the synagogue among the Writings and by the church among the Prophets. . . . That encourages two alternative readings of Daniel, as wisdom or as prophecy, as pedagogics or as eschatology, as halakah or as haggadah." That both are comprehended within Daniel indicates that each "alternative reading" must be asked to interpret the other.

[25]For further see Tim Meadowcroft, "Who are the Princes of Persia and Greece (Daniel 10)? Pointers towards the Danielic Vision of Earth and Heaven," *Journal for the Study of the Old Testament* 29 (2004): 99-113.

where there is resolution of temporal crises, when the hand of God is seen at work in contemporary events, two things should be remembered. The first is that this resolution and action foreshadow the promised resolution of all things. The second is to humility in the face of temporal success, and to ongoing loyalty and faithfulness. For there is yet more to come. And that "more" could entail suffering and mystery.

In the Meantime

In the meantime, like Daniel the reader is enjoined, however the paradox of wise participation is being experienced, to "go [his or her] way and rest" (12:13). For the story is not yet told, but God knows its ending. And Daniel and Daniel's people with him are participants in whatever that will be.

Old Testament Pedagogy on Mission

by Teresa Chai

Introduction

It is a privilege to be able to present an essay for this festschrift honoring Dr. Allison Kay Fountain. She is my Academic Dean, friend, dive instructor and sister in Christ. As an Old Testament scholar and academician, Fountain is an inspiration.

Here is an essay that adds a missionary track to Old Testament Pedagogy. In this survey of the Old Testament, since it will not be possible to cover everything remotely pedagogical and missional, an overview of the Law, Historical Books, Poetic and Wisdom Literature and the Prophets will be presented with attention to pedagogical and missiological implications.[1]

The Law

Genesis 1:27 states, "So God created man in his own image, in the image of God he created him; male and female he created them."[2] Several implications arise from this verse alone. First, God created all people groups, as well as both genders, along with their cultures. Another implication is the deep theological truth that humankind is made in the

---

[1] Grant McClung, *Globalbeliever.com: Connecting to God's Work in Your World* (Cleveland, TN, Pathway Press, July, 2000), 21- 44.

[2] All Bible verses cited are in NIV.

Imago Dei or "image of God."[3] This meant that Adam was given authority by God. Adam names the animals and was left as a care-taker of the land.

In the law, God is established as the Creator of the heavens and the earth. He gives human beings the privilege to know Him, to have stewardship over what He has created and to pro-create (Genesis 1:1, 28; 9:1; 11:1-9).

God as Creator not only provides for physical life, but also for spiritual life, the salvation of humanity after the fall. Genesis 3:15 is known as the *proto-evangelium* (first gospel) of a promised Savior: "And I will put enmity between you and the woman, and between your offspring and hers; he will crush your head, and you will strike his heel." Commentators point out that Christ, being born of Mary, is the "offspring" of the woman; the phrase "he will crush your head" is referring to the ultimate victory when Christ will crush Satan's head; the phrase "you will strike his heel" indicates the suffering and death of Christ on the cross.[4]

Not long after Genesis 3, another step in God's Good News is taken when God calls Abram, later called Abraham (Genesis 12:1-3), and tells him that he and his descendants are blessed to be a blessing to all nations. "The Lord had said to Abram, 'Go from your country, your people and your father's household to the land I will show you. I will make you into a great nation, and I will bless you; I will make your name great, and you will be a blessing. I will bless those who bless you, and whoever curses you I will curse; and all peoples on earth will be blessed through you.'" While the people of God are the "covenant people,"[5] this covenant was not based on ethnicity as the nation of Israel was not yet formed. Abraham is the Father of Faith for all nations.

---

[3] Gerhard von Rad, *Genesis: A Commentary*, translated by John H. Marks, The Old Testament Library (Philadelphia: The Westminster Press, 1961), 56.

[4] Christopher West, *Theology of the Body Explained: A Commentary on John Paul II's Gospel of the Body* (Boston: Pauline Books and Media, 2003), 303.

[5] Dianne Bergant, *People of the Covenant: An Invitation to the Old Testament*, The Come and See series, (New York, Sheed and Ward, 2001), 1.

The books of the Law have some other exciting pedagogical and missional accounts. For example, the "power encounter" when Moses dealt with Pharaoh and the Egyptian magicians in Egypt, and the Red Sea crossing when Pharaoh's armies chasing the Israelites ended up drowning in the sea. God renewed the covenant with His people at Mount Sinai, which has references to "all the earth" and "the nations."[6] Interestingly, the first Passover meal included foreigners. God called Israel to be "a kingdom of priests and a holy nation," a mediator between Him and other nations (Exodus 9:13-16; 12:38, 48; 19:4-6).[7] The Law was written to include Gentiles. If these foreigners converted to worship Yahweh, they became covenant people with equal rights and privileges as the Jews (Leviticus 16:29; 17:8; 19:33).

After forty years of wandering in the wilderness, most of the rebellious and stiff-necked generation of people had died. It was the new generation that had the privilege of entering the Promised Land.[8] Even Moses did not get this privilege. Instead it was Joshua and Caleb with their families that entered the land. The time of being in the desert served as a major spiritual lesson, that even though there was unbelief in Israel, God's purpose to fill the world would still be fulfilled (Numbers 14:15-21). Moses left these words of wisdom to the new generation that entered into the Promised Land, that Yahweh " . . . defends the cause of the fatherless and the widow, and loves the foreigner residing among you . . . . You are to love those who are foreigners, for you yourselves were foreigners in Egypt" (Deuteronomy 10:18-19).

---

[6]Denzil R. Miller, *Power Encounter*, lecture notes for college division Assemblies of God, Malawi, 2007, 4.
[7]Eugene H. Merrill, *Kingdom of Priests: A History of Old Testament Israel* (Grand Rapids, Michigan: Baker Academics, 2008), 52-54.
[8]William D. Gibbs III, *Entering the Promised Land: Contentment at Last* (CreateSpace Independent Publishing Platform, 2015), 25-36.

History

Old Testament narratives have different levels of reality on which these accounts unfold. Overarching is always the meta-narrative, God at work, whether He is mentioned or not. The next level focuses on a particular person or group of people that God is dealing with. Finally, there is a level in which the narrative has lessons or principles that are timeless and universal. Principles can be gleaned from these historical books from Joshua to Esther since God was at work in the lives of His people. As stated by Postman, "Without a narrative, life has no meaning. Without meaning, learning has no purpose. Without a purpose, schools are houses of detention, not attention."[9]

In Joshua, the miraculous happened as God's people took possession of the land promised to them. The land was not handed to them on a platter but they had to fight for it (Joshua 13:6; 18:1-10). Following all their conquests, the people were given rest by Yahweh and lived threat-free for a while. God renewed His covenant twice under Joshua's leadership and the Israelites were commissioned to be a blessing to other nations (8:30-35; 24:1-27, 4:24). Their exploits became well known to famous Gentiles such as the Queen of Sheba (I Kings 10:6) and Naaman the Syrian (I Kings 5). Some Gentiles converted to Judaism such as Ruth the Moabitess and Rahab.

Even though they were commissioned, Israel was not really a blessing to the other nations. In Judges, the people were doing "what was right in their own eyes." They were not satisfied with God as their King. They wanted to be like the surrounding nations and sought for an earthly king. Their behavior brought great decline to their nation as portrayed in repeating cycles of apostasy, punishment, repentance and restoration. In spite of Gideon's declaration " . . . The LORD will rule over you," (Judges 8:23), in the very next chapter of Judges is the account of

---

[9] Neil Postman, *The End of Education* (New York, NY: Vantage Books, 1995), 7.

Abimelech who tried to be king. From a theocracy Israel became a monarchy.[10] It was the time of the kings, beginning with Saul who started out well but ended up miserably. Succeeding him was David who was promised an everlasting kingdom (2 Sam 7:16). His son Solomon built a temple of world renown. When he dedicated the temple, he prayed that it would become an international house of prayer for all the nations, a missional foreshadowing.

Poetic and Wisdom Books

In the Poetic and Wisdom books, God's people use choice words and expressions about their God, done in an excellent way through songs, stories, words of wisdom and poetry. Some of these also illustrate the heart of God for people all over the world—whether in highlands, lowlands or islands—people of the nations, with the ultimate aim to see all worship Yahweh. George W. Peters described the Psalms as, "one of the greatest missionary books in the world."[11] Peters pointed out that there are, " . . . more than 175 references with a universal theme relating to the nations of the world. Psalms 2, 22, 33, 47, 50, 66, 67, 72, 96, 98, 117 and 145 can be studied with rich applications to the mission of God's people in a pluralistic world."[12] Although some Psalms were not written by King David, at least half are estimated to be written by him, for him or related to him. King David was a charismatic leader.[13] He was definitely inspired by the Spirit and anointed to write as well as sing songs glorifying Yahweh. Before he became king, one incident in King David's life points to this anointing from the Spirit of God: he was selected to play his lyre for King Saul in order that "the evil spirit would leave him." (1 Samuel 16:14, 23)[14]

---

[10]*International Standard Bible Encyclopedia*, s.v. "Theocracy."
[11]George Peters, *A Biblical Theology of Missions* (Chicago: Moody, 1972), 115- 16.
[12]Ibid.
[13]Talmud, Shabbat 56b.
[14]Erwin W. Lutzer, *The Serpent of Paradise: The Incredible Story of How Satan's Rebellion Serves God's Purposes* (Chicago: Moody Publishers, 1996), 23-26.

Psalm 67 was one of the psalms sung for the Feast of Pentecost, a festival that is celebrated fifty days after offering of first fruits which falls at the beginning of the summer harvest season in Israel. As a result, this song says, "the land yields its harvest; God, our God, blesses us" (Psalm 67:6) and this has been interpreted to also refer to a "spiritual harvest," a gathering of peoples from the nations of the world. The whole of Psalm 67 rings true to the Aaronic blessing of Numbers 6:24-26 which was the rule and covenant blessing of God to the nations.[15] This spiritual harvest was actualized in Acts 2, as peoples from different nations came to Jerusalem and witnessed the power of the Holy Spirit. Therefore, "It is not without significance that this psalm was sung at the Feast of Pentecost. When one remembers that it was at the Feast of Pentecost that God was to pour out his Spirit on all flesh, . . . the connection of this psalm with the Feast of Pentecost and its missionary message is all the more remarkable."[16]

Throughout the Old Testament's Poetic and Wisdom Literature there are specific themes of "Kingdom" and "the fear of the Lord," particularly in the royal psalms, where these songs were used during a celebration of a king's anointing or coronation, heralding royal entrance and reign (e.g., Psalms 2, 18, 20, 21, 45, 72, 89, 101, 110, 132, 144).[17] The language used indicates a much bigger application than just an earthly reign by pointing to God Who is the King of kings over all the earth. The nations are called "the people of the God of Abraham" (Psalm 47:9). In Psalm 117, an explosive worship time is described as all the nations join in exalting Yahweh.[18]

In this literature there is an indication of finality when God's mission will be accomplished. This is found in the phrase "the day of the

---

[15]William D. Barrick, *Psalms, Hymns and Spiritual Songs: The Master Musician's Melodies, Psalm 67 – A Missionary Psalm* (Place: Publisher, 2006), 1-5.

[16]Walter C. Kaiser, Jr., *Mission in the Old Testament: Israel as a Light to the Nations* (Grand Rapids, Michigan: Baker Books, 2000), 31.

[17]Brevard Childs, *Introduction to the Old Testament as Scripture* (Philadelphia: Fortress Press, 1979), 515–517.

[18]Ibid.

LORD" (Psalms 1: 2; 18:18; 23:6; 27:4; 39:4; 42:8; 88:1; 110:5; 118:22-26; 128:5; 140:7).[19] The feel of this day is of eschatological anticipation, much in line with the eschatological mission motivation of Pentecostals. Psalm 118:22-26 prophetically states, "the stone the builders rejected has become the cornerstone" (verse 22). This once Rejected King is now crowned; "Blessed is he who comes in the name of the Lord" (verse 26). In between these verses is a prayer: "Lord, save us; Lord, grant us success!" (verse 25). This psalm was a projection to a time when the Christ would be rejected. His people would have to persevere until He returned. They had the hope of salvation and success.[20] In a nutshell, the Poetic and Wisdom Literature teaches that living in anticipation of the "day of the Lord" is a life of blessing, wisdom, justice and love (in Hebrew, *hesed*). God intends this quality of life to serve as an invitation for the nations to enter into this covenantal relationship with Him.

The Prophets

Looking back, Israel's history is one of repeated rebellion even though the nation was clearly in a covenantal relationship with Yahweh from the time of Abraham, as they were Abraham's descendants. They were blessed to be a blessing. They followed Moses, but only to a certain extent, as they still made the golden calf when Moses went up to Mount Sinai. Then came the era of the Old Testament prophets, who charged the people of God with a covenantal case in Micah 6:1-8. Their kings and all the subjects had breached the covenant and all would be judged. Even other nations were guilty and would be judged. Yahweh was the Creator and Judge of the universe.[21]

---

[19]M. Coogan, *A Brief Introduction to the Old Testament: The Hebrew Bible in its Context* (Oxford: Oxford University Press, 2009), 260.

[20]J. S. Wright, *Day of the Lord*, in *The New Bible Dictionary*, ed. Douglas, J. D. (Michigan: Inter-Varsity Fellowship, 1962), 296.

[21]Gleason L. Archer, Jr., *A Survey of Old Testament Introduction* (Chicago: Moody Publishers, 2007), 330-31; Robert B. Chisholm, Jr., *Interpreting the Minor Prophets* (Michigan: Zondervan, 1990), 134-52.

There was hope, however! The foretelling by the prophet Isaiah included the Suffering Servant. This Servant would be the ultimate atonement and sacrifice for everyone's sins, " . . . he will bring justice to the nations." (Isaiah 42:1).[22] Isaiah declared that the Servant would not only save Israel but also the Gentiles, "I will also make you a light for the Gentiles, that my salvation may reach to the ends of the earth" (49:6).[23] Likewise, he repeated Solomon's prayer that the temple would be "a house of prayer for all nations." (56:7). In a further reading of Isaiah, there were at least three broad implications that can be gleaned from this book. First, Israel was Yahweh's first choice as His agent " . . . they may proclaim my praise." (Isaiah 43:21); second, as the One who initiated outreach to His people, He was to be the focus of Israel's worship and message of the one true God in the midst of idolatry (Isaiah 44.6); and third, there was a universality about what Israel was to do, it was a mission to the nations (Isaiah 45:21; 49:6; 52:10; 56:7). [24]

As for other Old Testament prophets, their messages too were ones that saw Yahweh's triumph at the end, when His Kingdom would be restored and that people from different nations would be included among the redeemed. For Pentecostals, the Prophet Joel's prophecy of a universal outpouring of the Spirit upon all flesh so that all who called on the name of the Lord would be saved (Joel 2:28-32) was fulfilled in Acts 2. Comparing the two, "Acts 2 does not change or reinterpret Joel 2, nor does it deny that Joel 2 will have a literal fulfillment when the Holy Spirit will be poured out on the whole nation of Israel."[25] Another fantastic prophetic vision was to see an enemy country of Edom becoming a worshipping community of Yahweh in the future (Obadiah 21; Amos 9:11, 12). Daniel had an even bolder vision of God's people crushing all

---

[22]Edward J. Young, *The Book of Isaiah* (Grand Rapids: Zondervan, 1972), III, 353.
[23]Michael W. Goheen, *A Light to the Nations: The Missional Church and the Biblical Story* (Michigan: Baker Academic, 2011), 100-105.
[24]Chris Wright, "Truth With a Mission: Towards a Missiological Hermeneutic of the Bible," *Missiologic* No.2 (Nov. 2001): n.p.
[25]Arnold G. Fruchtenbaum, *Israelology: The Missing Link in Systematic Theology*, rev. (Tustin, Calif.: Ariel Ministries, 1992), 844-845.

other kingdoms and ruling with Him forever (Daniel 2:44; 7:18). Zechariah said that many nations together with Israel would become God's people among whom God would dwell (Zechariah 2:11). In a narrative form, the book of Jonah illustrates the great compassion of God upon a violent foreign nation that repents.[26]

Through the exile and other times when they had to leave their own country, Israel was spun in a centrifugal force and launched out to other nations such as Babylon and Egypt. During the "intertestamental period," as Jews were dispersed to other lands, they brought their faith in Yahweh with them and shared it with others. There were at least six distinct characteristics in the practices and beliefs of the Jews that were developed during this time period: (1) the establishment of the synagogue; (2) the observance of the Sabbath; (3) the translation of the Old Testament Scriptures into Greek; (4) the teaching of the concept of monotheism; (5) the practice of individual and community biblical morality and (6) the strong belief in the coming of the Messiah.[27] All of this led up to the New Testament era when the awaited Messiah does come although He was not recognized nor accepted by all Jews. This is called the "period of silence," which is broken by John the Baptist. Following are some lessons from specific prophets.

Both the Old Testament and New Testament address both the Jewish people and the Gentile nations. God is the God of all nations not just of Israel. The calling of Abram in Genesis 12:3 and then also reiterated in Genesis 18:18, was that "all families of the earth" and "all nations of the earth" would be blessed through him.

Now consider the prophets who were addressing Gentile nations. God was calling these nations to repentance such as in the case of the prophet Jonah going to Nineveh. Israel was to be a model for the other

---

[26]Francis E. Gigot, *Special Introduction to the Study of the Old Testament* (New York, BiblioBazaar, 2009), 189-202.
[27]Ian Barnes and Josephine Bacon, *The Historical Atlas of Judaism* (UK: Chartwell Books, 2011), 157-165. Practices and beliefs developed during the Intertestamental Period.

nations and an encouragement to turn to Yahweh. Later in the New Testament, Paul and Barnabas give the rationale for preaching the gospel to the Gentiles in Acts 13:47, quoting from the prophet Isaiah 49:6 that the people of God are to be "a light to the Gentiles."

Lessons on Mission in Jonah

The prophet Jonah stands as a representative of the nation of Israel. He was called to preach repentance to Nineveh, a Gentile nation that had done unspeakable atrocities to Israelites, a good reason for Israel to hate the Ninevites. At the same time, Israel had an exclusive and particularistic attitude that claimed Yahweh to be their God only. This traced back to the covenantal relationship Israel had through Abram. However, they missed the point of the blessing and that was to be a blessing to other nations. In order to get the full impact of the account of Nineveh, the prophet Nahum in his book outlines the gravity of God's word to this nation.

The book of Jonah begins with God commanding His prophet to get up and go the city of Nineveh. The reason given for this command was that that their wickedness had come up to the LORD mentioned in Jonah 1:1, 2. Jonah was to proclaim the Word of the LORD to Nineveh as they too were under the Law of God.

Jonah articulates what he knows about God to the sailors by stating that he is a Hebrew and that the God he fears is the Creator of heaven, sea and earth in Jonah 1:9. This is a description of God that these Gentile sailors could identify with and which indicates that God is sovereign over all peoples of the world. This is seen in other verses such as 2 Kings 19:15; Isaiah 37:16; 40:12; Jeremiah 10:11; Acts 4:24; 14:15; 17:24; 25 and Revelation 14:6, 7.

Even on the ship, Jonah's evangelistic message worked. The contrast is that the sailors earlier in the narrative had been calling upon their own gods (Jonah 1:5), but after Jonah's speech about Yahweh they then cried to the LORD and even feared Him exceedingly as well as offered a sacrifice and vowed to the LORD (Jonah 1:14-16). This event is cross referenced to Jonah's prayer in the stomach of the fish as he recalls those who cling to worthless idols. This literally means those who cling to the "vapor of emptiness" and who "forfeit the grace that could be theirs" (Jonah 2:2-10). Within this prayer Jonah promises the LORD to bring these offerings and vows as per the mariners in verses 9 and 10.

God repeats His command to Jonah that He gave in Jonah 1:3 in Jonah 3:2. Jonah is willing to obey God and he proclaims God's Word and the people of Nineveh did believe Jonah's proclamation (Jonah 3:4, 5). Therein lies the tension of the prophetic judgment and the proclamation of salvation. In the New Testament, the same is seen in the Apostle Peter's message in Acts 2:14-16 and the Apostle Paul's speech to the Athenians in Acts 17:14-31 where their messages were on God's judgment but as the people responded in repentance, they then introduced the message of grace.

Jonah describes the Ninevites as turning to God with the same term used when Israel turned from sin to God. This mass conversion reported in Jonah 3:5-9 is unprecedented in the history of Israel. Verse 10 states that when those in Nineveh turned from their evil ways, God relented and did not do what He said He would do. In the New Testament, Jesus refers to Nineveh as an example of repentance and recognition of God's message through Jonah. In contrast, the Jews did not recognize who Jesus was (Luke 11:30, 32 and Matthew 12:41). It would seem like the Gentiles trumped the Jews in repentance.

Why did the prophet Jonah disobey God in the first place? Was it for personal reasons? The indication is that Jonah knew who Yahweh was. He is "a gracious God, merciful, slow to anger and kind" and He would respond by relenting from sending punishment when people repent of evil. Jonah's anger was because he could not reconcile the fact that these Gentiles who were enemies of the Jews would be given the same mercy as Israel, as recorded in Jonah 4:1, 2.

Definitely God is concerned about people. He chided Jonah who was more concerned about a plant than about the salvation of Nineveh that has 120,000 people and even cattle. The LORD's question was, "Should I not be concerned about that great city?" Jonah 4:11.

Lessons on Mission in Joel

The next book of a Minor Prophet to be considered is Joel. Judgment is pronounced over both Israel, in Joel 1 and 2, as well as on Gentile nations that are in opposition to God's people. This message of judgment is softened by the fact of God's grace, salvation and His return. The pinnacle of this is the promise of the outpouring of God's Spirit upon all flesh regardless of age and gender, and perhaps even social status in Joel 2:28 and in Joel 3. In the Book of Acts, this prophecy was fulfilled on Pentecost as per Peter's application in Acts 2:16. In his sermon Peter quotes the whole chapter of Joel in verses 17-21 and continues to the terrible judgments in verses 30 and 31. He ends with hope that all can be saved if they call on God and this salvation comes out of Zion mentioned in verse 32. The Spirit is given to both Jews and Gentiles.

Pauline writings also rely on the Joel concepts of calling on the names of the LORD to be saved, the outpouring of the Holy Spirit upon all flesh and that salvation is for both Jews and Gentiles in his treatise of this in Romans 10:11, 12; I Corinthians 1:2 and Titus 3:5, 6. In summary, the apostles understood that Pentecost was the beginning of world missions by the grace of God and salvation was for all who called upon the name of the LORD.

The terrible judgments in Joel included the destruction of Jerusalem which could be prevented by the repentance of both people and priests as stated in Joel 2:12-17, through the graciousness and mercifulness of God described in verse 13. The fulfillment of the destruction of Jerusalem was in 70 B.C.

Lessons on Mission in Daniel

In the New Testament, Jesus often referred to Himself as "The Son of Man." This term is found prominently in the Book of Daniel.

The setting of the Book of Daniel is Babylon. This nation of Gentiles heard about Yahweh. Daniel's prophetic word to this nation was Yahweh was going to deal with them, not only Israel. The narrative part of this book puts Daniel and his three friends in the Babylonian Court mentioned in Daniel 1. These four men were taught as if they were Babylonian yet they remained true to Yahweh and enjoyed God's blessings. Daniel, in particular, rose in the government ranks to be the third person in-charge as seen in Daniel 1:2; 2:48, 49; 5:28 and 6:3-19.

One of the ways God used to give Daniel favor with Nebuchadnezzar is that Daniel could interpret his dreams (Daniel 2 and 4:7-24). As for the other three Jews, their unbending stance got them thrown into the fiery furnace. God proved himself real and they were delivered. The king realized who Yahweh was as the God of Israel by his own confession recorded in Daniel 3:28-30. Recorded in black and white is Nebuchadnezzar's letter to all people from different nations in Daniel 4. In this letter the king confessed that God is great, His "works are truth and his ways justice . . . " (Daniel 4:37).

Following Nebuchadnezzar is Belshazzar who came on the scene in Daniel 5. God wrote on the wall for him. Then there is Darius who was faced with God's miraculous deliverance of Daniel from the lions' den in Daniel 6:25-28. He, like the previous king, issued a letter to the nations telling them that Daniel's God is a living God. The final chapters of the Book of Daniel are about his own dreams while serving these kings.

To reiterate, the Book of Daniel is about missions to the nations. The action took place in a Gentile country and the kings of this country made statements about Yahweh to other countries. Daniel prophesied to these nations regarding how God would deal with them and he introduced the Son of Man who would come and save them. Nebuchadnezzar's dream and Daniel's visions were about future ruling countries and the Son of Man who would come to save the world. The book is a contrasting of the kingdoms of this world and the kingdom of God.

Some popular interpretations are that the statue and the four beasts represent Babylon, Medes and Persians, the Greeks and the Romans. God replaces the kingdoms of this world with His kingdom. A stone destroys the statue and grows into a "great mountain and filled the whole earth" as described in Daniel 2:35, 45. In the later part of Daniel more details are given. The kingdoms end and the Son of Man ascends to heaven receiving "dominion and glory, and a kingdom" as well as "all people, nations and languages . . . serve him" in an eternal kingdom as stated in Daniel 7:14, 27.

From the Old Testament to the New Testament

It is important to see the interface of the Old Testament with the New Testament. In many ways the lessons taught in the Old Testament have been applied in the New Testament. Interestingly, the apostles quoted Jesus' commandment after Pentecost in Act 1:2 and 10:42 but they did not recite the Great Commission. Is that because the early church agreed on this so much so there was no need to quote it? Yet, in actuality, cross-cultural missions had a slow start in the early church. It did not really take off until Peter's encounter with Cornelius and his household of Gentiles. There was also controversy on this matter of outreach to Gentiles as seen in the Jerusalem Council of Acts 15 and the Epistle to the Galatians.

However, what the apostles gleaned about preaching the gospel to all the world is both from the teaching of Jesus and the Old Testament. To justify doing missions, the apostles quoted the Old Testament. Although the Great Commission was a fulfillment of the New Testament, this was the plan of God from the beginning, now fully implemented by the church. A clear example of this is found in Romans 15. The same teaching that the people of God were blessed of God to be a blessing to other nations was used repeatedly to justify evangelizing Gentiles. This teaching began in Genesis 12:3; 18:18; 22:17; 26:4; and 28:14, with application in Luke 1:54, 55, 72; Acts 3:25, 26; Romans 4:13-25; Ephesians 3:3,4 and in Hebrews 6:13-20; 11:12.

In Acts 13:46-49, Paul and Barnabas were rejected by the Jews in Antioch. They quoted Isaiah 49:6 that God has called His people to be a light to the Gentiles and bring salvation to the ends of the earth. They were going to preach the gospel to the Gentiles. Then in the Council in Jerusalem, it was James the Elder who quoted Amos 9:11 and 12 that Paul had the right to preach to the Gentiles as recorded in Acts 15:13. There is also cross-reference to Isaiah 61:4; Psalms 22:27 and 28 and Zechariah 8:22.

The Apostle Peter in Acts 10:42 and 43 said, "all the prophets witness that through his name whosoever believes in him shall receive the forgiveness of sins" when he preached the gospel to Cornelius and his household. Luke's Gospel has a different rendering of the Great Commission which draws from the Old Testament (Luke 24:44-49):

> He said to them, "This is what I told you while I was still with you: Everything must be fulfilled that is written about me in the Law of Moses, the Prophets and the Psalms." Then he opened their minds so they could understand the Scriptures. He told them, "This is what is written: The Messiah will suffer and rise from the dead on the third day, and repentance for the forgiveness of sins will be preached in his name to all nations, beginning at Jerusalem. You are witnesses of these things. I am going to send you what my Father has promised; but stay in the city until you have been clothed with power from on high."

Conclusion

There are many lessons to learn about the mission of God in the Old Testament. The teachings and narratives of the Old Testament repeatedly portray the Gentile nations as objects of God's salvation and care and welcome citizens of His kingdom. The Great Commission to God's people to share the Good News to the ends of the earth was first clearly stated in the Old Testament. Without the Old Testament, the apostles would have had little foundation for understanding God's mission in depth or justifying the cost. Without the Old Testament there is no New Testament.

Profiles of Contributors

Tim Bulkeley, PhD, was a Baptist Pastor in England, and Old Testament teacher in Congo and New Zealand. He has a passion for bringing the Old Testament to life online and face to face. He has lectured in a Bible School in a refugee camp as well as at universities and seminaries.

Deborah (Debi) Cassuto has been a part of the Tel Burna Excavation Project from the very first day of surveying in 2009. She is presently completing her PhD at Bar Ilan University on the textile tools from Iron Age Tell eṣ-Ṣâfî/Gath. Debi's publications cover gender and household weaving, textile production in the Iron Age Levant, and the finds at Tel Burna.

Teresa Chai, PhD, was a missionary to Bangladesh for eight years. She is an ordained minister with the Assemblies of God Malaysia. Presently, Teresa is a faculty member and administrator at the Asia Pacific Theological Seminary (APTS) in Baguio City, Philippines, currently filling the John Bueno Chair of Intercultural Studies. In March, 2018, she succeeded Kay Fountain as the academic dean at APTS.

Jacqueline N. Grey, PhD, is Associate Professor of Biblical Studies at Alphacrucis College, Australia and is currently church planting in West Asia. Her research interests include Pentecostal hermeneutics and prophetic literature.

Dave Johnson, DMiss, has been a missionary to the Philippines since 1994. He currently serves as a faculty member at APTS as well as the managing editor of the *Asian Journal of Pentecostal Studies* and the director of APTS Press.

Adelina C. Ladera, DMin, currently serves as the National Director of Christian Education Department of the Philippines General Council of the Assemblies of God.

Wonsuk Ma is a former academic dean at APTS and currently serves as Distinguished Professor of Global Christianity and PhD Program Director at Oral Roberts University, Tulsa, Oklahoma, USA.

Tim Meadowcroft, PhD, teaches Old Testament Studies and Biblical Interpretation at Laidlaw College in Auckland. His most recent work is a series of articles on a contextualized reading of the book of Daniel. He is also an assistant priest in his local Anglican parish of Henderson.

Chris McKinny, PhD. His dissertation focused on the historical geography and archaeology of the town lists of Judah and Benjamin in the book of Joshua. He is also a core staff member of the Tel Burna Archaeological Project.

Lian Sian Mung, PhD, is the senior pastor of Chicago Zomi Community Church in Wheaton, Illinois.

Itzhaq Shai is Senior Lecturer and Director of the Institute of Archaeology at Ariel University. Since 2009, he has directed the Tel Burna Archaeological Project. His publications cover the southern Levant in the Bronze and Iron Ages.

Shih-Hung (Benjamin) Yang is a supervisor assistant of Area B1 at Tel Burna.

Tham Wan Yee has been the President of APTS since 2009. He was a pastor of Canaan Assembly of God for over 18 years in Kuala Lumpur and has served as the Central District Superintendent of the Assemblies of God of Malaysia before joining APTS as a faculty member in 2004.

www.ingramcontent.com/pod-product-compliance
Lightning Source LLC
Chambersburg PA
CBHW051925160426
43198CB00012B/2041